The Shakespeare Cookbook

31

The Shakespeare Cookbook

Andrew Dalby and Maureen Dalby

THE BRITISH MUSEUM PRESS

© 2012 Andrew Dalby and Maureen Dalby

Andrew Dalby and Maureen Dalby have asserted the right to be identified
as the authors of this work

First published in 2012 by The British Museum Press
A division of The British Museum Company Ltd
38 Russell Square, London WC1B 3QQ

britishmuseum.org/publishing

A catalogue record for this book is available from the British Library

ISBN: 978-0-7141-2335-6

Designed by Simon Daley at Giraffe Books

Printed in China by C&C Offset Printing Co., Ltd

The papers used in this book are natural, renewable and recyclable products and the
manufacturing processes are expected to conform to the environmental regulations of
the country of origin.

The vast majority of the prints and objects illustrated in this book are in the collection
of the British Museum. The registration numbers and donor information for these
works are given in the corresponding captions. You can find out more about these and
other objects in all areas of the British Museum's collection by visiting the Museum
website: britishmuseum.org/research/search_the_collection_database.aspx

Frontispiece Globe artichoke. Drawing from an album by Jacques Le Moyne. *c.* 1585.
Watercolour and bodycolour, 20.6 x 14.5 cm. British Museum, PD 1962,0714.1.33,
purchased with assistance from the Pilgrim Trust and the Art Fund.

Contents

Preface

The period between 1564 and 1616 saw a wealth of publishing on the subject of food. For this reason we were able to take the decision to use wholly contemporary sources, both for the original recipes and for the writings about food that are cited in this book. We have quoted a few recipes from Mrs Sarah Longe's *Receipt Booke*, a manuscript of about 1610; one from the *Commonplace Book* of Lady Catherine Grey, who died a prisoner in 1568; and one recipe by Sir Kenelm Digby, who was a young man in Shakespeare's heyday but whose recipe book was only published after his death. All the other texts quoted here were not only known in Shakespearean times but were in print during his lifetime.

So we can say with full confidence that when Shakespearean characters talked about food, these are the very foods that they were talking about. The illustrations, too, are of objects and works of art created during the period, mostly drawn from the collection of the British Museum. Reconstruction archaeologists, and all others who work on food history and social history, will, we hope, find useful information and one or two surprises in this book (the Shakespearean breakfast menu, for example).

Our modern recipes have a specific purpose. They are not intended for dedicated reconstructors but for the majority of readers who may want to taste the same flavours that Shakespeare's audiences tasted – and meanwhile to think about health, nutrition and diet in the way that Shakespeare's contemporaries did. We haven't supplied modern versions of chaldron of swan (page 130) or poached pike (page 126), which few are now likely to reproduce. On the other hand, one or two sixteenth-century food ideas are so simple that we did not even need to give a modern version – as with the slices of orange, sprinkled with sugar, that were a fashionable novelty at banquets (page 137). Unless stated otherwise, our modern recipes are for four people.

Among the various books consulted (see the Further Reading on page 141), we should especially mention our use of the late Alan Davidson's *Oxford Companion to Food* and the work of Ken Albala,

'Vanity of vanities, all is vanity': young amorous couple at a richly decorated table.
Print after David Vinckboons, published in Haarlem in 1620. Engraving, 18.1 x 25.6 cm.
British Museum, PD 1857,0613.557.

Joan Fitzpatrick and Gilly Lehmann. When quoting Elizabethan food
and recipe books we have used the early printed texts, supplemented
by the online copies hosted at archive.org and at Google Books. We
have also found several modern editions and transcriptions useful,
the work of Rachel Doggett, E. Dever Powell, Daniel Myers, Johnna
Holloway, Sam Wallace, Mark and Jane Waks, Abigail Weiner and
Thomas Gloning.

   For easy reading the spelling in quotations has been modernized,
though the titles of the original recipes have been left in their original
spelling. The titles of cookbooks also appear in their original spelling.
Shakespeare's plays and other publications of that period have been
given their common modern names.

Introduction

I wonder if anything like this ever happened.
Author writing, –
'To be or not to be, that is the question:
Whether 'tis nobl–'
'William, shall we have pudding to-day, or flapjacks?'

Oliver Wendell Holmes, *The Poet at the Breakfast Table* (1872), p. 10

Shakespeare and food

William Shakespeare, born in Stratford-upon-Avon in 1564, married
to Anne Hathaway and with three children by 1585, must, at some
date not very long after that, have begun to spend much of his time
in London, acting and writing for the theatre. His name became
known gradually. A certain 'shake-scene', a so-called 'upstart crow',
was attacked in a pamphlet by rival dramatist Robert Greene in 1592.
Shakespeare's long poem *Venus and Adonis* was printed in 1593. *Titus
Andronicus*, first to be published of all the plays now attached to his
name, appeared in 1594. In 1598 'William Shake-speare' began to be
credited on the title pages of plays, and in that same year the author
Francis Meres described Shakespeare as 'the most excellent' among
English writers of comedy and tragedy.

Meres lists among Shakespeare's successes two plays that we draw
on in this book, *Romeo and Juliet* (see chapter 1) and *Henry IV part 1*

(chapter 2). Some of his greatest work lay in the future. *The Merry Wives of Windsor*, *Twelfth Night* (chapter 3) and *Hamlet* (chapter 4) appeared in or before 1602, *Macbeth* (chapter 5) and *The Winter's Tale* (chapter 6) in or before 1611. *The Taming of the Shrew* is difficult to date. *King Henry VIII* (chapter 7), on which Shakespeare probably collaborated with John Fletcher, was a fairly new play when its most famous performance took place on 29 June 1613. This was when a discharge of firearms, required off-stage during the banquet scene, led to the burning down of the Globe Theatre.

Shakespeare died in 1616. His popularity grew slowly in the seventeenth and early eighteenth centuries, more rapidly thereafter, and with no significant interruptions. He is the world's most performed playwright.

Food was important to Shakespeare, whether he was conscious of it or not. There are feast and banquet scenes in several plays, including some that we might have used here and have not. In practically every play in which such scenes are used, the feasts and banquets are central to the development of the plot. In *Romeo and Juliet*, one of Shakespeare's earliest works, it is at the supper and masked ball at the Capulets' that the intruder Romeo first meets Juliet. In *King Henry VIII*, one of his last, it is at supper at Cardinal Wolsey's that the masked Henry dances with Anne Boleyn. At the wedding feast in *The Taming of the Shrew* Petruchio and Kate, having got it together just in time, win the competition. In *Macbeth* the king's command to Banquo – 'Fail not our feast!' – is, to his horror, obeyed: Banquo has meanwhile been murdered but his ghost attends the feast. In *The Winter's Tale* it is at the sheep-shearing feast that hidden identities are revealed. In *Henry IV part 1* at the Boar's Head Tavern the ambush is concocted, and in *Henry IV part 2* during the outdoor meal in Shallow's orchard Falstaff learns of the death of Henry IV. The first incident will prove Falstaff's incompetence or cowardice, while the second leads to his snubbing at the coronation: in both cases the groundwork of his future discomfiture is laid at a meal.

There are also suggestive mentions of feasts that don't take place on stage. We did not use the lavish meals hinted at in *Antony and Cleopatra*, though we take full advantage of the baked meats from Hamlet's father's funeral feast, served up cold (Hamlet sarcastically

View of London from the South Bank, as it appeared before the Great Fire of 1666, with London Bridge on the right, Southwark Cathedral in the foreground, the Globe Theatre (rebuilt after the 1613 fire; see page 125) to its left with flag flying, and old St Paul's on the opposite bank. 1610, published in John Speed's *The Theatre of the Empire of Great Britaine* (1611–12). Engraving, 7 x 14.6 cm. British Museum, PD Heal,Topography.71, bequeathed by Sir Ambrose Heal.

suggests) at his mother's wedding. Apart from feasts and banquets, all through Shakespeare's works there are frequent uses of food as metaphor and simile. Characters such as Sir John Falstaff and Sir Toby Belch define themselves in food terms and are so defined by others. Throughout this book incidental mentions of food in the plays will be quoted, and we could have chosen plenty more.

Food has been important to everyone, in all historical ages, but it is really true that the sixteenth century (which as far as England is concerned ends in the reign of Elizabeth) marks a significant period in food history. There are several reasons for this. London, a larger and more prosperous city than ever before, attracted trade in food (and other things, luxuries and essentials) from all over England, from the European continent, and from the whole of the known world. New foods from newly discovered lands were being rapidly added to the culinary repertory. And, as explained on page 139, the Shakespearean period marked a flowering in the English book trade, notable not least for the number of food books, texts on diet, and recipe books that were in print.

In spite of these developments, the way people thought about the contribution made by individual foods to human diet and health had not changed very much since Roman times. That was when the physician Galen and his Latin and Greek successors set out schematically how each food measured up on the scales of heat and moisture, how easily and quickly it was 'concocted' or assimilated into the body, and how it affected the four bodily humours.

Everyone believed in those scales. Whenever we talk about pepper being 'hot' (although we know that the thermometer would disprove it) and wine being 'dry' (though wine is notoriously wet) we are betraying the fact that somewhere at the back of our minds we still believe in them.

Everyone – at least, everyone who wrote about the subject – still believed in the four humours. They, too, formed part of everyone's vocabulary, used in discussing one's own temperament and that of others. The humours are blood, phlegm, yellow bile and black bile, and people are by nature sanguine, phlegmatic, choleric or melancholic, these temperaments being determined by a predominance of any one humour over the other three. Disease results from a temporary predominance of any humour.

How are these humours to be adjusted? The answer lies in the foods we choose to eat, in the spices and sauces with which we temper them, and in the medicines that doctors prescribe for us. Foods are less powerful in their effects (but we eat more of them); spices and herbs can be very powerful (but we don't take them in large quantities); medicinal concoctions are potentially the most powerful (and therefore the most dangerous if the doctor happens to get it wrong).

Looking at sixteenth-century health practices from a twenty-first-century point of view, we can say immediately that the humoral theory is mistaken: no such four humours determine our temperament. But we can also see why the theory continued to be believed. It's true that food choice affects one's health and constitution; it's true that spices and herbs can have powerful effects, often positive, occasionally negative; and it's true, too, that medicinal concoctions are potentially the most effective of the three but also the most dangerous.

Although, in Shakespeare's time, the old theories were still universally accepted, the seeds of change were being sown. Medieval traditions were beginning to fall from favour. Scientific methods were encouraged by Galen and other ancient scientists whose original works were now being rediscovered and translated. Experimentation on new foods and drugs discovered in Asia and the Americas had begun to throw up difficulties with humoral theory, difficulties that would eventually lead to its abandonment. These were exciting times.

Meals and mealtimes

Breakfast, the first meal of the day, was taken soon after dawn. Country people in winter breakfasted before dawn to take full advantage of the hours of daylight. A typical breakfast was a meal so light that it hardly seemed to be a meal at all; hence, unlike other meals, there would be no need to say grace beforehand. In *Henry IV part 1* Falstaff jokes about what Prince Hal will do when he succeeds to the throne, and whether he should be called 'your Grace', but no, it will have to be 'your Majesty' –

'for grace thou wilt have none –'
'What, none?'
'No, not so much as will serve to be prologue to an egg and butter.'

This is good material for the food historian. First, it tells us that the average member of the audience did not say grace as a prologue to breakfast ('What, none?'); second, it gives us two of the typical constituents of a late sixteenth-century breakfast in London, because if this was not typical, Shakespeare's audience would fail to recognize its own breakfast in five syllables of a fast-paced dialogue. The same breakfast menu is repeated when carriers spending the night at an inn at Rochester on the Canterbury road are said to be 'up already, and call for eggs and butter, and will be away presently'. Admittedly the egg and butter won't make a healthy breakfast on their own, but with the help of our imaginations we can easily add to the menu the staple food – bread – and the staple drink, ale for Londoners and Kentishmen, sack for Sir John (see page 24). A fuller breakfast menu ('butter and cheese and umbles of a deer') is found in Robert

Greene's *Friar Bacon and Friar Bungay*, printed a few years before the *Henry IV* plays; this nourishing breakfast is offered to a party of noblemen who have ridden through the night, and they have the cheek to demand 'a bottle of wine' to go with it.

There are no invitations to breakfast in Shakespeare, but there are invitations to dinner, which for many people marked the end of a long morning's work. Dinner was the main everyday meal, and it was a midday meal. Shakespeare happens to make the timing clear both in *Measure for Measure* when Escalus, told that it is eleven o'clock, invites the Justice 'home to dinner with me'; and in *As You Like It* when Rosalind says to Orlando:

Breakfast, by Diego Velázquez. *c.* 1617. Oil on canvas, 183 x 118 cm.
The State Hermitage Museum, St Petersburg.

I must attend the Duke at dinner. By two o'clock
I will be with thee again.

If we read this too closely with Andrew Boorde's *A Compendyous Regyment* we will suppose that the duke dined shortly before one o'clock, because Boorde instructs that 'an hour is sufficient to sit at dinner'; but that is to take texts more literally than is wise. Perhaps the duke had more leisure than Boorde's average reader, and sat longer at his dinner. Other texts confirm that most people began to dine at twelve or a little before.

Some, including Boorde, took the view that dinner should be the longer meal: one should sit 'not so long at supper', he says severely. William Bullein in *The Government of Health* directs a special warning to those who are 'phlegmatic' (in whose temperament phlegm predominates): late suppers, 'specially if they be long', are followed by painful nights. The general view among dietary authors is that supper should be eaten five or six hours after dinner. The view among speakers in Shakespeare's plays is slightly different: they are almost unanimous that supper comes at night, which should usually mean after six o'clock. We get more detail on just one occasion, in *Richard III*, when Catesby tells the king: 'It's supper-time, my lord. It's nine o'clock.' This, again, we should not read too literally. The king's life may not be as regular as most people's – he is about to be killed, after all – and he is sufficiently preoccupied to reply 'I will not sup tonight', possibly the only explicit reference in Shakespeare to a missed meal.

As a Shakespearean character you don't invite people to breakfast. You may invite people to dinner informally, on the spur of the moment; if you do, your dinner will still not be wholly unlike your dinner on the day before. Supper is quite a different matter. You will invite people to an evening entertainment, on a more formal and planned basis than your dinner invitations. You may name it a feast, a supper or a banquet, and all these names will be true, and your family supper on this particular day will be transformed. There will be a supper (i.e. an evening meal not unlike dinner, but bigger and more elaborate than the dinner you had a few hours earlier). There may be music and dancing. Towards the end of the evening, before or after or among the dances, there will be a banquet. A banquet is not so much a whole and distinct meal; it may sometimes appear to be a dessert course attached to supper. It is probably a buffet, probably consisting partly of finger food; complicated to make, elaborate to display, easy to eat, somewhat playful – though not usually as insubstantial as the magic banquet in *The Tempest* which was tantalizingly laid out by spirits under Prospero's command and removed again before anyone had a chance to taste it.

Notes on some ingredients

Pepper, in this book, is black pepper, which was imported to Europe from southern India. It was exotic and fairly expensive, although the 'India route' around Africa, opened up by the Portuguese, had reduced prices by breaking the old monopoly of Arab and Italian traders. Attempts were being made to identify cheaper substitutes, not only in West Africa (Benin pepper) but also in Central America (the 'hot', red or chilli pepper that Columbus and his successors were so pleased to find). Chilli peppers, though agreed by dieticians to be equally hot, were easily distinguished from the real thing; in any case they had not yet reached England. Shakespeare never mentions any of the alternatives to pepper, but if you can get them it would not be inappropriate to try long pepper or cubebs (already available in ancient and medieval times) or Benin pepper (a novelty on the English market in the 1590s) as an alternative seasoning to black pepper.

Ginger, imported from India and Eritrea, had been well known in Europe for about 1500 years. 'Razes of ginger' – roots, that is – are mentioned in *Henry IV part 1*. Among the health benefits of ginger Sir Thomas Elyot, in *The Castel of Helth*, mentions one that is not generally familiar: 'Being green, or well confectioned in syrup, it . . . quickeneth remembrance if it be taken in the morrow fasting.'

Cinnamon, extremely expensive and therefore much prized in traditional medicine, had become gradually cheaper and is called for in many recipes. In *The Haven of Health*, a lifestyle manual aimed at university students and their tutors, Thomas Cogan writes imprecisely that cinnamon is 'the bark or rind of a certain tree growing in the

Indies', specifically Ceylon (Sri Lanka), southern India and south-east Asia. Cogan adds a recipe for distilling a 'cinnamon water' or liqueur, adding: 'I reckon it a great treasure for a student to have by him in his closet, to take now and then a spoonful.' For students who wish to test this, liqueurs flavoured with cinnamon can still be found.

Nutmeg, still quoting Cogan's vague geography, is the 'fruit of a tree in India like unto a peach tree'. 'India' here means the Moluccas in eastern Indonesia. During the years of Shakespeare's success English merchants in the East Indies were engaged in an ultimately fruitless struggle with the Dutch for direct access to the producing islands. The great importance of nutmeg, as of the other spices, was in its health-giving and medicinal effects. For students 'that have weak heads', Cogan advised that nutmegs 'being taken last at night in a caudle of almonds or hempseed, they procure sleep'. Both the weak heads and the sleep may possibly have been an effect of the hempseed; we offer no modern recipe. Students are also advised 'if they can get nutmegs condite, which must be had of the apothecaries, that they would have always by them half a pound or more to take at their pleasure'. 'Condite' means conserved in syrup, like ginger root: we have not yet encountered nutmeg in this form. Sir Thomas Elyot adds that nutmeg 'comforteth the power of the sight, and also the brain, in cold dyscrasies'.

Mace, the husk of the nutmeg fruit, is more commonly called for in Elizabethan recipes than in modern ones. If you can't get it, a smaller quantity of nutmeg can be used as a substitute: the flavour is not wholly different. Cogan regards mace, often sold in whole pieces, as 'to the stomach very commodious and restorative, being used in meats; and for this purpose they are boiled whole in broths or cullises [*coulis*] or milk'.

Sugar – the sugar cane, that is – originated many millennia ago from a hybridization of two grass species in New Guinea. Its usefulness ensured its spread across the world in cultivation; by the medieval period it was grown in parts of the Middle East. In Shakespeare's time it had already been planted in the West Indies, but the supply of white granulated sugar came to England from Cyprus, Crete, Rhodes,

Sicily and Madeira. Loaves of 'sugar candy', both white and brown, were also familiar. Sugar was much sought after as a medicine, regarded as more wholesome than honey. Sugar was very popular in food among those who could afford it, but it was not yet by any means the cheap product we know today.

The seeds of **caraway**, **anise** and **fennel**, closely related and with similar health effects, were well known to Elizabethan cooks and dieticians. 'Caraway breaketh wind', as William Langham writes in *The Garden of Health*, and Thomas Cogan confirms it: 'I advise all students that be troubled with wind in the stomach or belly to cause fennel seeds, anise or caraway to be wrought up in their bread' (mixed with the dough). Caraway comfits, that is, caraway seeds coated in sugar, were often eaten alongside apples, which were regarded as difficult to digest. A plate of caraway seeds was handed out in Judge Shallow's orchard in *Henry IV part 2* for exactly this reason. The seeds make an excellent digestive to nibble after a meal, like fennel seeds in an Indian restaurant – and fennel seeds of course have the same effect on the digestion, as Cogan again confirms: 'Students may use [fennel seeds] made up in comfits, wherein I myself have found great commodities, as being often grieved with windiness of the stomach.'

Mustard, like the three seeds just mentioned, legitimately counts among spices although its origin is not exotic. It was familiar across Europe and was a food of which England was proud. 'His wit's as thick as Tewkesbury mustard', Falstaff says of Poins, and the reference to this Gloucestershire town is confirmed in Cogan's *The Haven of Health*, which adds that good mustard came also from Wakefield in Yorkshire. Cogan has much to say about mustard. It is especially useful to 'such students as be heavy headed and drowsy, as if they would fall asleep with meat in their mouths'; it not only 'procureth appetite, and is a good sauce with sundry meats both flesh and fish', but is also 'medicinable to purge the brain'. Cogan's logical demonstration of this claim is amusing: 'If a man lick too deep, it straightway pierceth to the brain and provoketh neezing, which extremity may be soon helped by holding bread at your nose so that the smell thereof may ascend up to the head.' Finally he recommends mustard in pill form to music scholars:

The Sense of Taste, by Jan Brueghel and Peter Paul Rubens. 1618.
Oil on panel, 64 x 109 cm. Museo del Prado, Madrid.

[Mustard and honey pills.] If any be given to music and would fain have a clear voice to sing, let them make mustard seeds in powder and work the same with honey into little balls, of the which they must swallow one or two down every morning fasting, and in short time they shall have very clear breasts.

Padua was one of the European cities renowned for its mustard. The Italian cookbook *Epulario*, republished in Venice in 1596 just about the time when *Romeo and Juliet* was first seen on the London stage, gives a recipe for Padua-style mustard followed by another for mustard pills: here the idea is for the traveller, who requires mustard for gastronomic or health reasons, to take it with him dry to be mixed when needed:

To make good Paduan mustard. Take the mustard, grind it very well, take raisins and grind them as well as you can, have some breadcrumbs and a little red sanders and cinnamon, and a little verjuice (or vinegar and grape juice) to add liquid to the mixture, and press it through a sieve.

To make mustard that you can carry in pieces. Take the mustard, grind it as above, take raisins very well ground, and add to these ingredients cinnamon and a little cloves; make round pills or little square pieces of whatever size you like, and put them to dry on a table. When dried you can take them from place to place as you want. Note that when you wish to take or use them you can mix them in a little verjuice or vinegar or vino cotto or grape juice.

Vinegar, 'the corruption of wines whether made from grapes, fruit or grains . . . is developed rather for use in flavouring or to excite the palate and the appetite', writes Charles Estienne in 1550, incidentally confirming that wine vinegar, cider vinegar and ale vinegar were all familiar to him; 'it is useful in that by its acidity it corrects the blandness or excessive sweetness of foods'. Estienne adds practical advice: 'To be useful and effective vinegar should not be new but clear, and should retain the flavour of the wine from which it is made. Add it to sauces, salads and salty foods, sparingly, so that it lends nothing to them except its flavour.'

A method for making vinegar is offered in an unpublished recipe collection of Shakespeare's time, part of the *Commonplace Book* of Lady Catherine Grey:

To make vyneger. Take old wine drawen from the lees; put it into a vessel and set it in the sun. Then take oatmeal and water and temper them together and make it in cakes and bake them in an oven till they be dry; then break them hot in small pieces and put them into the wine with a bag of elderflowers dried. Then let it stand in the sun 14 days and it will make pure vinegar. If your vessel be great you must put in the greater quantity of these things.

Verjuice is the acid juice of unripe grapes. It was often used in France and Britain as an ingredient to add sourness to a sauce; less often now, though it can still be found. The ease of making and using lemon juice is probably what drove verjuice off the market, and if you can't get verjuice then lemon juice will serve as a substitute, though the flavour is not the same. The following instructions, for a lightly fermented verjuice and for a flavoured type, are from the Italian cookbook *Epulario*:

To make verjuice. Pick grapes of the wild variety called usiglie, or unripe grapes, and crush them very well dry, adding a little salt; have at hand a small quantity of old verjuice to pour on them; pass through a sieve.
To make verjuice with fennel. Take some garlic if you like it, and the sweetest and best fennel flowers you can get, and cook and crush them very well together. Add dill to new verjuice and pour it on the crushed herbs; pass through a sieve; add a little salt when necessary.

In England grapes did not grow wild, and cultivated grapes were far too valuable to be picked before they were ripe. Hence, as Thomas Cogan tells us, in England at that period verjuice was made of 'crabbes' – crab-apples, that is – 'pressed and strained'. A young man faced with marrying for money discusses his future wife's finer points with his servant in Thomas Middleton's *Women Beware Women*:

'Methinks, Sordido, she has but a crabbed face to begin with.'
'A crabbed face? That will save money.'
'How? Save money, Sordido?'
'Ay, sir, for having a crabbed face of her own, she'll eat the less verjuice with her mutton: it will save verjuice at year's end, sir.'
'Nay, an your jests begin to be saucy once, I'll make you eat your meat without mustard.'

Two varieties of **rose water** were familiar in Tudor England, as Cogan explains: 'The red rose water pure, without any other thing mingled, is most commended for wholesomeness, but the damask rose water is sweetest of smell.'

Two kinds of **oranges** were already known in England at this period. Bitter or Seville oranges had been imported for some centuries, while sweet oranges were a new thing and highly popular among those who could afford them. Oranges were not grown in England – heated orangeries were still in the future – but were imported by sea from

Spain. Although oranges travel better than many other fruits, buyers were often disappointed when an orange that looked perfect turned out to be past its best, dry and tasteless.

Sir Thomas Elyot strongly recommends as medicine the candied peel of oranges, which 'comforts the stomach', and the juice 'eaten with sugar, in a hot fever'. He also gives a recipe for an orange relish:

[Orange sauce.] The juice of oranges having a toast of bread put unto it, with a little powder of mints, sugar, and a little cinnamon, maketh a very good sauce to provoke appetite.

Lemons, which were also imported by sea, were candied and their juice was made into a syrup. Like oranges, they were strongly favoured by the dietary writers. Thomas Cogan suggests a morning medicine:

[Morning draught.] A cup of Rhenish or white wine, with a lemon sliced and sugar, is a pleasant medicine next a man's heart in a morning.

Sweet potatoes were known in England by the date of *The Good Huswifes Handmaide for the Kitchin* but they were a 'fortifying' medicine, not an everyday food item. They are required in that 1594 cookbook in an aphrodisiac concoction. We quote the original recipe but offer no modern version of this courage-provoking tart:

A tarte to provoke courage either in man or woman. Take a quart of good wine, and boil therein two burr [burdock] roots scraped clean, two good quinces, and a potato root well pared and an ounce of dates, and when all these are boiled very tender, let them be drawn through a strainer, wine and all; and then put in the yolks of eight eggs and the brains of three or four cock sparrows, and strain them into the other, and a little rosewater, and seethe them all with sugar, cinnamon and ginger, and cloves and mace, and put in a little sweet butter, and set it upon a chafing-dish of coals between two platters, and so let it boil till it be something big.

Thomas Elyot confirms that sparrows as a foodstuff 'stir up Venus (and particularly the brains of them)'.

The usual household drink, for all who had the resources to produce it at home, was **ale**. Bottled ale also existed, for city dwellers who had no time to make it themselves and enough money to buy it. Beer, distinguished from ale by being flavoured with hops, was not yet commonly made in England and is mentioned by Shakespeare only as 'small beer', a weakly alcoholic drink suitable for children. Cider (see page 134) was familiar only in the West Country. Mead and metheglin (see page 90) were known as Welsh specialities, though appreciated by some in England for their health benefits.

Wine in Shakespeare's England was imported, hence expensive. According to Gervase Markham, writing in 1613, no wine at all was made in England in his time: the growing of grapes 'is but only for a fruit-dish at our tables, for neither our store, nor our soil, affords us any for the wine-press'.

The best known table wines were Rhenish and Gascon. Both of these travelled by river barges and then seagoing ships to reach London and other English cities. Rhenish wines, so called because they came by way of the Rhine and the North Sea, corresponded to the German and Alsatian wines of today. Gascon (or Bordeaux) and Rochell wines reached England by sea from the ports of Bordeaux and La Rochelle on the Bay of Biscay; these wines were produced for the most part in former English possessions in Poitou and Gascony in south-western France.

Rhenish wine was mostly white; French wines were white, red and claret, but claret did not yet mean 'red Bordeaux wine' as it does now. In Shakespeare's time claret was any light-coloured red wine; in French it was usually called *vin vermeil*, although the French term *clairet* is also sometimes used in this sense. William Bullein, in his 1579 book on health, describes it carefully as 'pure claret, of a clear jacent [hyacinth] or yellow colour; this wine doth greatly nourish and warm the body, and it is an wholesome wine with meat'.

Bullein's expression 'pure claret' is intended to distinguish this from clary, which was a medicinal wine with added spices and sugar, called *claré* (occasionally *ipocras claré*) in sixteenth-century French. This was less well known than its relative, ipocras (see recipe and explanation on page 42), a spiced white wine sweetened with sugar.

Wines that reached England from further south were all fortified, but not by adding spirits to them at the end of the fermentation process as is done now. The normal method of fortification was by adding sweet grape juice or grape syrup; the result would still, as now, be a wine that was stronger than the average, sweeter than the average, and less likely to spoil. Such wines were suited to slow, long-distance transport: table wines could scarcely survive the rough and wearisome sea journey from the Mediterranean. About a dozen regional styles of fortified wine were imported to sixteenth-century England.

Names occurring in just a few sources include bastard, which came from southern Portugal and is appropriately called for in the recipe for fists of Portingale (page 55). It was a sweet wine, possibly a distant relative of port; the variety name *bastardo* is still in use in Portugal. Malaga, still familiar as a sweet, heavy white wine, is named in a play by Shakespeare's contemporary Thomas Middleton (page 98). But the best known of all these fortified wines were certainly Malmsey, Canary and sack.

Malmsey was a grape variety from Crete and the Aegean islands (*monemvasiós*) and a style of fortified wine, strong in residual sugar but with pleasing acidity, whose export trade once centred on the Greek port of Monemvasia. It had been familiar in England since the fourteenth century. The variety had by Shakespeare's time spread westwards along the Mediterranean coasts. Under a variant name (*malvasía*) it already flourished on Lanzarote and La Palma in the Canary islands; the wine from there, however, was familiarly known as **Canary** or Canaries. It is mentioned in *Twelfth Night* and in *Henry IV part 2*: 'You have drunk too much Canaries, and that's a marvellous searching wine, and it perfumes the blood ere one can say, what's this?' The Malmsey grape was also one of those that had begun to flourish on Madeira. Shakespeare mentions **Madeira** wine once – in *Henry IV part 1* Falstaff is accused of selling his soul to the devil for 'a cup of Madeira and a cold capon's leg' – but in English texts of this period no link is visible between Madeira and Malmsey.

Sack was a strong and relatively dry white wine from the southern coasts of Spain. It was as popular among Queen Elizabeth's courtiers as it was at the Boar's Head Tavern. In 1604 Elizabeth's Scottish successor James I, aiming to economize, ruled that the 'sergeant of our cellar' should issue no more than twelve gallons of sack a day for consumption at court. The best sack was known as 'sherris sack', meaning that it came from Jerez ('Sherris') de la Frontera. Although the exact style of sack may be impossible to recreate now, it's hard to deny a probable resemblance between sherris sack and dry reserve sherry (see also page 46).

As regards bread: **manchet**, **cheat** and **maslin bread** are explained on page 31. **Sippets** were slices, often triangles, of bread. Richard Surflet in *The Countrie Farme* wrote of 'sippets or small slices of bread dried upon the coals' – toast, in other words. A **coffin** is a pie shell: see the recipe and explanation on page 80. For **sops** see the recipe on page 102.

A **trencher** was no longer a thick slice of bread used instead of a plate, as it often was in the previous century when Caxton published his translation of Virgil's *Aeneid*. '*Etiam mensas consumimus*' – we are even eating our tables – said the boy Ascanius when the Trojans first set food on Italian soil: they had no plates and so little food that, after setting out all that was left on flatbreads, they finished the meal by eating up the bread. So, as Caxton tells the story, 'they set themselves at dinner, and made trenchers of bread for to put their meat upon'.

By the late sixteenth century a trencher was usually a wooden platter, square or circular, on which food was served – an everyday item in most houses. 'I found you as a morsel cold upon dead Caesar's trencher,' says Antony to Cleopatra in the Shakespeare play. A trencher was the simile that came first to the mind of Captain John Smith, explorer and settler of Virginia, when he was discussing the world view of the native Americans he encountered: 'They imagined the world to be flat and round, like a trencher, and they in the midst.'

Wooden trenchers from the British Museum's collection are illustrated in this book. So is a **posset cup**, whose purpose was to allow the liquid at the bottom to be drunk before the curd at the top had all been eaten. Kitchen equipment mentioned in the recipes includes a **pipkin**, a small earthenware pot or pan.

A banquet with musicians and servers (detail). Print by an anonymous Italian artist, c. 1520–1600. Woodcut, 27.2 x 37.6 cm. British Museum, PD 1877,0609.336.

'Save me a piece of marchpane!'

ROMEO AND JULIET

The 'ancient feast' and masked ball at the Capulets' were at the root of it all. As a kindness to a messenger who can't read, Romeo spells out the list of guests, and remarks:

'A fair assembly: whither should they come?'
'Up.' 'Whither to supper?' 'To our house.' 'Whose house?' 'My master's.'
'Indeed I should have asked you that before!'
'Now I'll tell you without asking. My master is the great rich Capulet, and if you be not of the house of Montagues, I pray come and crush a cup of wine.'

If he hadn't generously read out the guest list he wouldn't have been rewarded with this dangerous invitation; Mercutio wouldn't have persuaded him to accept it; he wouldn't ever have visited the Capulets' to dance and 'crush a cup of wine'; he wouldn't have met

Juliet and would doubtless still have been uselessly in love with the unfriendly Rosaline.

The messenger who can't read and the intervention of Mercutio are Shakespeare's innovations, but when the tragedy was first performed, around 1591, the story of Romeo and Juliet was already popular. It had spread to France, and then England, soon after its first appearance in a little book with a none-too-catchy title published at Venice in 1530, *Historia novellamente ritrovata di due nobili amanti*, the 'newly rediscovered story of two noble lovers'. That first version is set in Verona in the days of Bartolommeo della Scala, who ruled the city briefly from 1301 to 1304. It already has a hero named Romeo, a member of the Montecchi family, and a heroine named Giulietta of the Cappelletti.

In that early version the story opens with the Verona *carnevale*,

annual festivities that mark the end of winter and the beginning of Lent. Antonio Cappelletti gives a supper and masked ball (this fits nicely with what we know of Verona in 1530, not so well with the years 1301–4). The Montecchi and the Cappelletti are at daggers drawn, but, just as in Shakespeare's *Romeo and Juliet*, Romeo is tempted to attend: he hopes to get a glimpse of the lady with whom he is in love. Once he arrives in the ballroom she is, of course, forgotten: he sees Giulietta, and from that moment onwards his eyes are fixed on her. He persuades friar Lorenzo da Reggio to marry them secretly. This and the family enmity bring about their deaths.

Wooden trenchers, one painted with pears (opposite), the other with medlars. Made in England, *c.* 1600. Diam. 13.6 cm. British Museum, P&E 1896,0807.8.i & k, given by Augustus Wollaston Franks.

Among Shakespeare's additions to the story are the amusing incidents surrounding the 'ancient feast', the banquet and masked ball at the Capulets'. There is byplay among the servants clearing away after supper –

'Where's Potpan, that he helps not to take away? He shift a trencher? He scrape a trencher?'
'When good manners shall lie in one or two men's hands, and they unwashed too, 'tis a foul thing.'
'Away with the jointstools, remove the court-cupboard, look to the plate. Good thou, save me a piece of marchpane!'

Potpan's job, which he evidently wasn't doing, was to help clear away the remains of the meal and scrape clean the trenchers (wooden platters). The portable furniture has to be moved aside to give room for dancing; this includes any stools and also the court-cupboard or sideboard from which dishes had been served during supper. We notice that care is needed not to damage the silverware while the court-cupboard is being shifted.

There are more lively details later, in the preparations for Juliet's arranged marriage to Paris (a marriage that can never happen, because by this time she and Romeo are secretly married). Old Capulet and his wife bustle ineffectively:

'Hold! Take these keys, and fetch more spices, nurse!'
'They call for dates and quinces in the pastry.'
'Come, stir, stir, stir, the second cock hath crowed.
The curfew bell hath rung, 'tis three a clock.
Look to the baked meats, good Angelica,
Spare not for cost.'

'Baked meats' (see page 80) was a general term for pies, whether or not they contained meat.

Bread

Bread was the basic food of Elizabethan England. There were several kinds. Manchet, said Gervase Markham in 1615, was 'your best and principal bread' and it was made of wheat flour alone. For cheat, another kind of wheat bread, the flour was 'bolted through a more coarse bolter than was used for your manchets'. These two correspond to modern white and light brown bread, while a third kind, 'the coarsest bread for man's use', resembled modern wholemeal bread. This everyday bread would include the wheat bran (called 'chissel' in the first recipe below) and was often based on other cereals than wheat, depending on what might be cheap locally.

Things were not always so simple: in the Royal Household there was a kind of bread between manchet and cheat, called 'cheat fine'. It may perhaps have resembled the sugary 'fine bread' for which a recipe is given overleaf. Whatever it was, it is listed in the provisions for the Prince of Wales's table in 1610: 'For the Prince his highness' breakfast: manchet, 2; cheat fine, 2; cheat, 4; beer, 3 gallons; wine, 1 pitcher; beef, 1 service; mutton, 1 service; chickens, 2.'

Writers on diet had their own opinions about the different kinds of bread. Thomas Elyot, for example, knew all about the digestive effects of bran: 'Bread having much bran filleth the belly with excrements and nourisheth little or nothing but shortly descendeth from the stomach.' Elyot's advice was different from that of modern nutritionists. He concluded that a light brown bread, 'the mean between both, sufficiently leavened, well moulded and moderately baken is the most wholesome to every age'.

The making of fine manchet. Take half a bushel of fine flour twice bolted, and a gallon of fair lukewarm water, almost a handful of white salt, and almost a pint of yeast, then temper all these together, without any more liquor, as hard as ye can handle it: then let it lie half an hour, then take it up, and make your manchets, and let them stand almost an hour in the oven. Memorandum, that of every bushel of meal may be made five and twenty cast of bread, and every loaf to weigh a pound, beside the chissel.

The Good Huswifes Handmaide for the Kitchin (1594)

To make fine bread. Take half a pound of fine sugar well beaten, and as much flour, and put thereto four egg whites, and being very well beaten, you must mingle them with aniseeds bruised, and being all beaten together, put into your mould, melting the sauce over first with a little butter, and set it in the oven, and turn it twice or thrice in the baking.

Thomas Dawson, *The Good Huswifes Jewell* (1596)

December: courtyard of an inn with a woman baking bread (detail). Print from a series of the Twelve Months, by an anonymous French artist, *c.* 1580. Woodcut, 18.1 x 28.6 cm. British Museum, PD E,9.174.

Wheat and rye loaf

In Lancashire and Yorkshire, says Thomas Cogan, household bread in winter was made from mixed wheat and barley. Rye bread, familiar 'almost throughout this Realm' according to Cogan, was not praised by the dietary writers. Consider William Bullein's opinion on the subject when baking this modern recipe – 'Rye bread is windy and hurtful to many: therefore it should be well salted and baked with aniseeds' – and then recall that, according to Cogan, rye was not so bad when mixed with wheat. The mixture was called 'maslin bread' and it was 'much used in divers shires, especially among the family'. Hence our choice here – but this can be easily varied if readers prefer a different blend.

500 g/1 lb 2 oz wheat and rye flour (the ratio depends on the baker)
2 teaspoons salt
400 ml/14 fl oz/1³/₄ cups tepid water
1 teaspoon brown sugar
2 rounded teaspoons dried yeast
Extra flour for dusting

Sieve the flour and salt into a large mixing bowl and leave to stand at room temperature while preparing the yeast mixture. Put 80 ml/3 fl oz/¹/₃ cup of tepid water into a measuring jug, stir in the sugar and yeast, then leave for 10 minutes. Stir once.

Make a well in the centre of the flour and pour in the yeast mixture with a wooden spoon, then gradually add the remaining 320 ml/10³/₄ fl oz/1¹/₃ cups of water. Finish incorporating the flour into a smooth dough with your hands. Knead well until springy. Leave the dough to rise, covered with a tea towel or clingfilm, for about half an hour.

Knock back the dough and knead for a further 5 minutes. Cut the dough in half and form each into rounds, put on a floured baking sheet and let the dough prove again for 45 minutes.

Meanwhile preheat the oven to 230°C/450°F/gas mark 8. Bake for 10 minutes, turn down the heat to 180°C/350°F/gas mark 4 for a further 30 minutes.

Capon with oranges or lemons

Capons – male chickens castrated and fattened – were and still are a delicacy, bigger and more succulent than their sisters. They made a heavy meal, one particularly suitable for Sir John Falstaff, for example (see chapter 2). 'The flesh of all birds is much lighter than the flesh of beasts', wrote Thomas Elyot in his little dietary handbook. 'The capon is above all other fowls praised, forasmuch as it is easily digested and maketh little ordure and much good nourishment. It is commodious to the breast and stomach.' The early recipe that follows seems to recall modern Greek taste in serving a chicken with a sauce that contains egg and lemon.

The oranges required here (see also page 21), imported from Spain, are probably bitter or Seville oranges.

To boyle a Capon with Orenges or Lemmons. Take your capon and boil him tender and take a little of the broth when it is boiled and put it into a pipkin with mace and sugar a good deal, and pare three oranges and peel them and put them in your pipkin, and boil them a little among your broth, and thicken it with wine and yolks of eggs, and sugar a good deal, and salt but a little, and set your broth no more on the fire for quailing, and serve it without sippets.

A Book of Cookrye (1591)

Chicken with egg and lemon sauce

4 chicken joints
50 g/2 oz butter
2 sliced onions
2 sliced carrots
2 tablespoons chopped fresh dill or 1 tablespoon dried dill
350 ml/12 fl oz/1$\frac{1}{2}$ cups water
Salt and pepper

For the sauce:
30 g/1 oz cornflour
2 tablespoons cooking liquor
Juice of 1$\frac{1}{2}$ lemons
2 eggs

Lightly brown the chicken pieces in the butter in a casserole. Add the vegetables, dill and seasoning, along with the water. Cover and cook for 1$\frac{1}{2}$ hours in the middle of the oven at 180°C/350°F/gas mark 4.

Near the end of the cooking time prepare the sauce by combining the cornflour and cooking liquor in a small bowl. In a saucepan beat the eggs before adding the cornflour mixture. Add the lemon juice, blending well.

At the end of the cooking time remove the chicken from the casserole and keep warm on a serving dish. Gently introduce tablespoons of the cooking liquor to the sauce over a low heat. Stir until the sauce thickens (you will not need all of the liquor in the casserole). Some of the vegetables can be included if you wish.

Pour the sauce over the chicken and serve.

Medlar tart

Medlars are an ancient European fruit. The tree is irregular and angular in growth, with large fleshy leaves and beautiful white blossom in late spring. The fruit itself is not unlike a small apple, bronze-coloured, round, containing five large seeds. It is rather unprepossessing – very hard, almost inedible, and very astringent (as Henry Lyte puts it in *A New Herbal*, 'Medlars do stop the belly, especially being yet green and hard'). Then in late autumn, around the time of the first frost, the fruit begins to rot; hence the line in *As You Like It*: 'You'll be rotten ere you be half ripe, and that's the right virtue of the medlar.' But medlar-lovers don't say 'rot', they say 'blet'. It can be picked just before this stage and stored. If not picked already, when the fruit turns dark brown and soft it must be harvested at once: it is suddenly 'more convenient to be eaten', as Lyte says, and the flavour is unique. According to Thomas Elyot, 'they may be eaten after meals as a medicine, but not used as meat, for they engender melancholy'. We have not found this. The flesh of the fruit can be scooped out and mixed with cream and sugar to eat fresh – there is nothing more heavenly – and also made into conserves.

A medlar has a large blossom end, surrounded by sepals, inside which the segments can be seen, each containing a seed. This very distinctive feature, which immediately distinguishes it from an apple, gave the medlar its Anglo-Saxon name 'open-arse' and the scarcely less vulgar sixteenth-century variant 'open-tail'. These names were familiar enough, and suggestive enough, for Mercutio to play on them in *Romeo and Juliet*. He imagines Romeo in Juliet's orchard:

Now will he sit under a medlar tree,
And wish his mistress were that kind of fruit
As maids call medlars, when they laugh alone.
O Romeo that she were, O that she were
An open etcetera, thou a poperin pear.

The first quarto – not a trustworthy text – has the words exactly as printed here: later editions have 'or' instead of 'etcetera'. Neither version fits the metre, and it's not clear what the actor would do: perhaps a cough would fill the space and suggest the crucial word. The image, in any case, is quite plain: the medlar or Juliet, open to receive the long-shafted poperin pear or Romeo.

Medlars. Drawing from an album by Jacques Le Moyne. c. 1585. Watercolour and bodycolour, 21.4 x 14.3 cm. British Museum, PD 1962,0714.1.34, purchased with assistance from the Pilgrim Trust and the Art Fund.

To make a Tarte of Medlers. Take medlars that be rotten, and stamp them, then set them on a chafing dish and coals, and beat in two yolks of eggs, boiling it till it be somewhat thick, then season them with sugar, cinnamon and ginger, and lay it in paste.

Thomas Dawson, *The Good Huswifes Jewell* (1596)

Medlar tart

We recommend this as an open tart which can be served with cream. One could cover the tart in a meringue made from the 2 egg whites and browned for a further 15 minutes.

At least 12 bletted medlars
2 egg yolks
Caster sugar to taste
Pinches of ground cinnamon and ground ginger
1 quantity of shortcrust pastry (see page 81)

Line a 35-cm/14-inch pie dish with the shortcrust pastry. Bake blind for 20 minutes in an oven at 180°C/350°F/gas mark 4. When cooked, reduce the heat to 170°C/325°F/gas mark 3.

Cut the medlars in half and scoop out the soft flesh with a teaspoon. Warm the flesh in a small saucepan, with sugar to taste and the spices. Blend in the beaten egg yolks and continue to stir over the heat to thicken slightly.

Tip the medlar mixture into the flan case and put back into the cooler oven for a further 15 minutes.

Marchpane

'Save me a piece of marchpane!', one servant calls to another as they are clearing the remains of the banquet at the Capulets'. Marchpane was a stiff almond paste 'made of very little flour', Gervase Markham explains, 'with addition of greater quantity of filberts, pine nuts, pistaches, almonds, and rose sugar'. It could be moulded into a hard (but edible) cake as a centrepiece for a dessert table, and it cried out to be decorated. 'Garnish it with pretty conceits, as birds and beasts, being cast out of standing moulds', says Hugh Plat in *Delights for Ladies*, adding that caraway seeds, good for the digestion, could be sprinkled on before icing – yes, it was iced. It could also be gilded with edible gold leaf.

Marchpane originated in Italy, where its name was *marzapane*. It burst into English history, we believe, at a very Shakespearean moment. The courtship of Henry V (Falstaff's Prince Hal) and Catherine de Valois, amusingly enacted in *Henry V*, was followed in real history by a feast in London on 24 February 1421 celebrating Catherine's coronation. The full menu is recorded by an assiduous chronicler, Robert Fabyan. There is not room for it all here, but the third course ended with a spectacular subtlety: 'A marchpane garnished with diverse figures of angels, among the which was set an image of Saint Catherine holding this reason: *Il est escrit, pur voir et dit, per mariage pur cest guerre ne dure*' (or, in English, 'It is said and written for all to see: holy wedlock will end this war').

In 1561–2, just before Shakespeare was born, Queen Elizabeth I received three presents of marchpane. One, made by George Webster, her master cook, took the form of a chessboard (alternate squares perhaps being gilded); a second, from Richard Hickes, Yeoman of the Chamber, was 'made like a tower, with men and sundry artillery in it'; a third, from John Revell, Surveyor of the Works, was a replica of the old St Paul's church.

In the eighteenth century, long after Shakespeare's time, marchpane began to be made with a softer texture, no longer as a cake in its own right but as the coating for rich fruit cakes that we know today as marzipan.

Latiné   AMYGDALAE.
Gallicé   AMANDES.
Anglicé   ALMONDES.

Branch of an almond tree (detail). Print from a series after Jacques Le Moyne, published in Paris in 1586. Hand-coloured woodcut, 7.3 x 6.4 cm (image). British Museum, PD 1952,0522.1.46, bequeathed by Sir Hans Sloane.

To make a marchpane. Take half a pound of blanched almonds, and of white sugar a quarter of a pound; of rose water half an ounce, and of damask water as much. Beat the almonds with a little of the same water, and grind them till they be small; let them on a few coals of fire till they wax thick, then beat them again with the sugar, fine. Then mix the sweet waters and them together, and so gather them and fashion your marchpane . . . Then having white paper underneath it, set it upon a warm hearth, or upon an instrument of iron or brass made for the same purpose, or into an oven after the bread is taken out, so it be not stopped, it may not bake but only be hard and thorough dried. And ye may while it is moist stick it full of comfits of sundry colours in a comely order. Ye must moist it over with rose water and sugar together. Make it smooth, and so set it in the oven or other instrument: the clearer it is, like lantern horn, so much the more commended. If it be thorough dried, and kept in a dry and warm air, a marchpane will last many years. It is a comfortable meat, meet for weak folks such as have lost the taste of meats by reason of much and long sickness. The greatest secret that is in the making of this clear, is with a little fine flower of rose, rose water and sugar beaten together and laid thin over the marchpane ere it go to drying: this will make it shine like ice, as ladies report.

John Partridge, *The Treasurie of Commodious Conceits* (1573)

Marchpane

200 g/7 oz almonds
120 g/4 oz icing sugar
2–3 tablespoons rose water
Glacé fruit to decorate

Grind the almonds in a pestle and mortar, adding a little rose water to moisten. Add the sugar gradually and mix well, alternating with the remainder of the rose water. Gather the mixture together and press into a round tin, 20 cm/8 inches in diameter, lined with rice paper or greaseproof paper. One can decorate with glacé fruit. Glaze at this point (or, if preferred, ice after baking) with 1 tablespoon each of icing sugar and rose water mixed together. Bake in a preheated oven at 160°C/325°F/gas mark 3 for about 30 minutes or until the marchpane has hardened. It keeps well. Pieces can be broken off and used as a sweet.

Ipocras

The idea of spiced wine goes back to classical Roman times and it is still familiar today. Think of ginger wine; think of vermouths such as Martini and Noilly Prat, which are spiced wines with a very clear line of descent from ancient recipes. Wormwood was originally included in those recipes for the very specific reason that it is a vermifuge (it kills intestinal worms). They went on being made because they helped the appetite. Thomas Cogan recommends all students to keep a 'rundlet' of three or four gallons of vermouth 'which they may draw within their own chambers, as need requireth'. Lucky students.

No one who drinks vermouth nowadays chooses to do so because they think they have worms, or because wormwood 'strengtheneth a weak stomach and openeth the liver and spleen', as Cogan asserts. They choose it because they like the taste. Spices and spiced drinks have benefited from this dichotomy for thousands of years. They are thought to be good for you (and, with all the usual caveats, they do sometimes offer health benefits) but they also taste good.

Ipocras or ypocras was the most popular spiced wine of the fifteenth and sixteenth centuries. Its name is clearly connected with the legendary ancient Greek physician Hippocrates, and probably comes from the fact that a 'Hippocratic bag' or sock, *chausse d'Hippocras*, longer and narrower than a modern jelly bag, was used to allow the wine to filter through the spices. Hence a 'bag' is specified in the 1591 recipe given here.

A few recipes for red ipocras exist (in 1555 in the *Tresor d'Evonyme Philiatre* for example). Usually, however, ipocras is said to be white, and its most distinctive feature was that, instead of easily available honey, it contained exotic white sugar (which was regarded as a medicinal spice as much as a culinary one).

To make Ipocras. Take a gallon of wine and an ounce of cinnamon, two ounces of ginger and a pound of sugar, twenty cloves bruised and twenty corns of pepper gross beaten, and let all those soak one night, and let it run through a bag.

A Book of Cookrye (1591)

[Wormwood wine.] Steep a branch or two of common wormwood in half a pint of good white wine, close covered in some pot all night, and in the morning . . . strain it through a clean linen, and . . . put in a little sugar and warm it, and so drink it.

Thomas Cogan, *The Haven of Health* (1636)

Ipocras

Ipocras is usually based on white wine and flavoured with sugar. A version made with red wine was once called pyment. If you use mead you are producing a version of metheglin, but the true method for metheglin is different (see page 90).

Take 3 bottles of dry white wine of not too heavy a flavour (say, muscadet), 250 g/9 oz of cane sugar, and about 1 tablespoon each of ground or well-crushed spices, selecting any 3 or 4 of these: ginger or galangal, cinnamon, pepper or long pepper or cubebs, mace or nutmeg, cloves, cardamom, melegueta pepper, or others that you wish to try. Mix the sugar and spices with the wine in a jug or bowl. Cover with clingfilm and let it stand for at least two hours: for the sake of the wine this period should be fairly brief, which is why ground spices are preferable. Pour the spiced wine into clean bottles through a filter paper (for a small quantity a piece of kitchen towel can be folded like filter paper) in a conical funnel. Seal the bottles and store in the dark. Store for at least 2 days before using; it will be better after 2 to 3 weeks.

It is best to avoid pink peppercorns and any mixes that include them. Spices based on capsicum (cayenne, paprika, etc.) were not yet available in Shakespeare's England; star anise and Sichuan pepper were unknown; coriander, cumin and anise were not sufficiently exotic for inclusion in ipocras. These aside, the logic behind the choice of spices is not so much the flavour but the health benefit.

When making a herbal wine, as in Thomas Cogan's recipe opposite, know your herbs. Wormwood, to take that as an example, is poisonous not only to worms but also to humans if used in excessive quantity.

Pottery jug found at Arleigh, near Colchester, Essex. 15th or 16th century. H. 13.2 cm. British Museum, P&E 1867,1014.1, given by Kenneth R.H. Mackenzie.

Feasting peasants
seated at a table
before a cottage
(detail). Print after
David Vinckboons,
c. 1600. Engraving,
10.6 x 16.9 cm.
British Museum,
PD 1847,0318.67.

'The dinner attends you'

FALSTAFF AND FRIENDS

In performing *Romeo and Juliet*, Lord Hunsdon's Servants had a free hand with the northern Italian city of Verona – luckily for them, because they knew no more about the place than their audiences did. Around 1598 the same company (now called the Lord Chamberlain's Servants) presented their chronicle play *The History of Henry the Fourth*, and this time they were more constrained. The action centres on London, Windsor Castle and the Kent Road as far as Rochester; these were real places familiar to many members of the audience. If this was a problem for the writers and players, their solution to it was uncompromising: they embraced realism. You can picture the ambush site at Gadshill at least as clearly as the hapless Falstaff could see it in the darkness. You can almost name the inn at Rochester in whose yard one carrier says, 'The turkeys in my pannier are quite starved', and another replies, 'I have a gammon of bacon and two razes of ginger to be delivered as far as Charing Cross'.

Turning to London, the most amusing scenes take place in a tavern

that really existed and that a good many of the audience must have known well, the Boar's Head in Eastcheap. Admittedly the Boar's Head had not been there in Henry IV's time. In the sixteenth century, however, it was a familiar landmark – lively enough to welcome Sir John Falstaff and his unruly crew, not to mention Doll Tearsheet, who efficiently seduces the fat knight in the sequel play *The Second Part of Henry the Fourth* – but also respectable enough that Prince Hal could be imagined visiting the tavern when, advised by Poins, he sets out in search of his old friend:

'Where sups he? Doth the old boar feed in the old frank?'
'At the old place, my lord, in Eastcheap.'
'What company?'
'Ephesians, my lord, of the old church.'
'Sup any women with him?'
'None, my lord, but . . . Mistress Doll Tearsheet.'

Gritty realism can scarcely go further than Poins riffling through the pockets of the snoring Falstaff. They find 'one poor pennyworth of sugar-candy' and an unpaid bill:

'Item a capon. 2s. 2d. – Item sauce. 4d. – Item sack two gallons. 5s 8d. – Item anchovies and sack after supper. 2s 6d. – Item bread. ob.'
'O monstrous! But one halfpennyworth of bread to this intolerable deal of sack?'

That, then, was the menu for a long and expensive dinner at the Boar's Head. Sack, undoubtedly Sir John's favourite wine, was strong dry wine from southern Spain. We would probably recognize it as belonging to the sherry family, and would surely enjoy it even more after studying Sir John's health advice:

A good sherris sack has a twofold operation; it ascends me into the brain, dries me there all the foolish and dully and crudy vapours which environ it; makes it apprehensive, quick, forgetive, full of nimble, fiery and delectable shapes; which delivered over to the voice . . . becomes excellent wit. The second property of your excellent sherris is the warming of the blood, which before, cold and settled, left the liver white and pale, which is the badge of pusillanimity and cowardice; but the sherris warms it, and makes it course from the innards to the parts extremes. It illumines the face, which, as a beacon, gives warning to all the rest of this little kingdom, man, to arm; and then the vital commoners and inland petty spirits muster me all to their captain, the heart, who, great and puffed up with this retinue, does any deed of courage. And this valour comes of sherris.

No wonder he needed two gallons a day of it. The character of Falstaff – 'that huge bombard of sack, that stuffed cloakbag of guts, that roasted Manningtree ox with the pudding in his belly' – as triumphantly developed by the Lord Chamberlain's Servants and their

Alloy tavern token from the Boar's Head Tavern, Eastcheap, showing a boar's head with a lemon in its mouth. Issued in London, 1649–66. Diam. 1.5 cm. British Museum, CM 1911,1209.27.

staff writer William Shakespeare, allowed room for plenty of allusions to food and drink, gluttony and drunkenness. 'There's no more faith in thee than in a stewed prune', he unwisely tells the mistress of the Boar's Head, though behind her back he is more complimentary: 'Is not my hostess of the tavern a most sweet wench?' the prince asks, and Falstaff, evidently something of a classicist, replies: 'As the honey of Hybla, my old lad of the castle.' The sweet Sicilian honey of Hybla was a commonplace in Elizabethan poetry just as it had been in Latin long before.

Falstaff was the company's most popular creation of these years, blazoned on title pages on which Shakespeare himself hadn't yet earned a billing. The company played him chiefly for laughs, yet he was more than a mere figure of fun. On his visit to Judge Shallow's West Country orchard, in *Henry IV part 2*, Falstaff figures in a comic interlude that outgrows its origins. Shallow gives orders for a picnic ('Some pigeons Davy, a couple of short-legged hens, a joint of mutton, and any pretty little tiny kickshaws, tell William cook') and Falstaff, as if to his own surprise, enjoys it briefly.

The apples that Shallow shares out after the meal

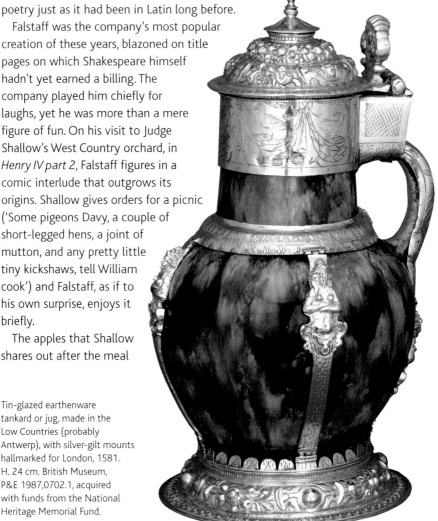

Tin-glazed earthenware tankard or jug, made in the Low Countries (probably Antwerp), with silver-gilt mounts hallmarked for London, 1581. H. 24 cm. British Museum, P&E 1987,0702.1, acquired with funds from the National Heritage Memorial Fund.

('There's a dish of leather-coats for you') are an omen, however. They ought to remind Falstaff of the apple-johns of Kent and an old joke of Prince Hal's, as retold for the audience by the barmen at the Boar's Head:

'What the devil hast thou brought there – apple-johns? Thou knowest Sir John cannot endure an apple-john.'
'Mass, thou sayest true. The Prince once set a dish of apple-johns before him, and told him there were five more Sir Johns; and, putting off his hat, said "I will now take my leave of these six dry, round, old, withered knights." It angered him to the heart; but he hath forgot that.'

Leathercoats and apple-johns were two tough-skinned old apple varieties that kept well. Modern mass-grown apples are often kept in cold stores for months, and some varieties emerge reasonably well from these conditions, but certain older varieties will keep for several months without chilling. An example is the Clochard of western France, which ripens in mid-autumn and will last at least until April in a cool room. To be kept in this way apples of suitable varieties (they will be thick-skinned and both sweet and acid) should be picked when on the verge of full ripeness. They must be taken straight from the tree, rejecting any fruits that are not perfect or whose stem broke off when picked, and they must not be dropped or bruised. We store them between layers of newspaper, which shields them from light, occasionally sorting them to remove any that begin to rot. Already in December they are sweeter than fresh-picked apples; by February the texture has begun to change, becoming crumblier, a bit like apple sauce. Like these, apple-johns and leathercoats would have been succulent, but wrinkled and freckled, in spring.

Falstaff has forgotten the apple-johns, and he is touchingly confident of a glorious future as he weighs the news of Henry IV's death and Hal's accession to the throne. Falstaff's fall is imminent. He is about to be rejected by his young friend; he will be snubbed at the new king's coronation.

Rabbit

In Shakespeare's time 'rabbit' was the name for the babies, 'cony' for the full-grown animal: hence a suggested menu in the 1591 *Book of Cookrye* includes 'two cunnies or half a dozen of rabbets: sauce mustard and sugar'. As shown by the original spelling, retained in this quotation, the word's usual pronunciation was 'cunny', which was also a rude word. When reading the Bible aloud it had become necessary to pronounce *cony* very carefully to avoid laughter in the audience. This conflict of senses is probably the reason why the word 'cony' was eventually replaced by 'rabbit'.

Rabbits were plentiful in Shakespeare's England. Those bought at market were sometimes taken from the wild but usually farmed; farm rabbits were, however, 'free-run', kept in warrens, not in hutches.

To 'smoor' in the recipe below was to smother and therefore to stew. In several modern languages words meaning 'smother' or 'stifle' have the culinary meaning of 'stew'. Sweet butter (like *beurre doux* in modern French) means fresh unsalted

Meat for the kitchen. Drawing by Frans Snyders, *c.* 1594–1605. Pen and brown ink with brown wash over charcoal, 23.3 x 42.7 cm. British Museum, PD T,14.11, bequeathed by William Fawkener.

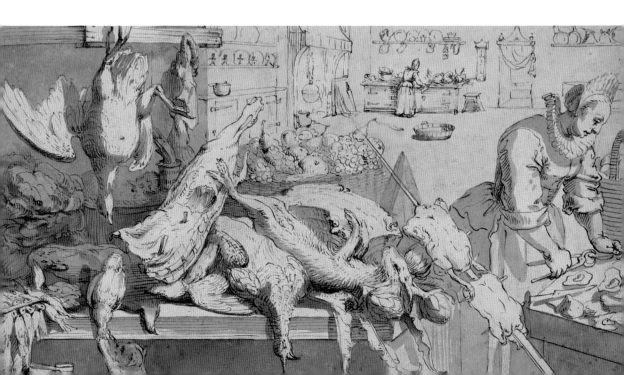

butter. Sippets, as explained in the introduction, are little triangles of fried or toasted bread. For verjuice, called for in this and many later recipes, see page 20.

To smoor an old coney, ducke, or mallard, on the French fashion. Parboil any of these, and half roast it; lance them down the breast with your knife, and stick them with two or three cloves. Then put them into a pipkin with half a pound of sweet butter, a little white wine verjuice, a piece of whole mace, a little beaten ginger, and pepper. Then mince two onions very small, with a piece of an apple, so let them boil leisurely, close covered, the space of two hours, turning them now and then. Serve them in upon sippets.

John Murrell, *A New Booke of Cookerie* (1615)

Rabbit with cider and mustard

4 rabbit joints dusted in flour
2 finely chopped onions
2 sliced carrots
300 ml/10 fl oz/1⅓ cups cider
4 whole cloves
1 teaspoon ground mace
1 teaspoon ground ginger
3 tablespoons crème fraîche
Olive oil, salt and pepper

Brown the rabbit pieces in oil in a pan before adding to a casserole dish. Gently sauté the onions and carrots for 5 minutes before adding to the casserole along with the cloves, mace, ginger, salt and pepper. Deglaze the frying pan with the cider and add to the casserole. Cover and cook for 1½ hours in the oven at 180°C/350°F/gas mark 4.

Then mix the crème fraîche and stir into the casserole. Continue to cook uncovered in the oven for a further 30 minutes. Serve the rabbit pieces smothered in the casserole sauce.

One could substitute 2 tablespoons of grainy mustard, in place of the spices, to flavour this dish in the 'French fashion' described in the original recipe. On mustard see page 18.

Capon in white broth

'Of all tame fowl a capon is most best', writes Andrew Boorde in his diet
handbook. Elizabethan dieticians worried themselves sick about onions,
however. Early authorities said that they 'engender ill humours and corruptible
putrefactions in the stomach and cause fearfull dreams'. And yet it was
noticeable that ordinary working people, who knew nothing about the dietary
rules, ate onions heartily and seemed to be all the better for it. Thomas Cogan
therefore recommends onions to the students for whom his *Haven of Health*
is written. He favours onion sauce with mutton, woodcock and capons, and in
general onions cooked in good broth; hence the following recipe would have his
full support. 'Being used in pottage, or otherwise boiled for sauces (as cooks best
know) or baked in a pie, as I have seen in some places, they be not hurtful but
wholesome', Cogan insists.

To boyle a capon in white broth. Boil your capon in fair liquor, and cover it
to keep it white, but you must boil no other meat with it; take the best of the
broth, and as much verjuice as of the broth, if your verjuice be not too sour, and
put thereto whole mace, whole pepper and a good handful of endive, lettuce or
borage, whether of them ye will, small raisins, dates, marrow of marrow bones, a
litle stick of cinnamon, the peel of an orange. Then put in a good piece of sugar,
and boil them well together. Then take two or three yolks of eggs sodden, and
strain them and thick it withal, and boil your prunes by themselves, and lay upon
your capon: pour your broth upon your capon. Thus may you boil anything in
white broth.

The Good Huswifes Handmaide for the Kitchin (1594)

Chicken in white broth

When invited to meals with our nearest French neighbours we eat simple food,
straight from the farm. A chicken is cooked in a pan of water along with onions,
carrots, leeks and seasoning. Potatoes are added half an hour before cooking
time is over. The chicken is removed along with the leeks and potatoes to be
kept for the main course; the broth is served as an entrée with the addition of
vermicelli.

In the following version remove the chicken and some broth, to be used in the fricassee recipe (below). The remainder of the broth and vegetables are served as a potage with the addition of vermicelli, just as our friends would do.

1 chicken (kept whole)
2 onions
2 carrots
2 leeks
1 cinnamon stick
1 teaspoon whole peppercorns
Peel of an orange (not grated)
Enough water to partly cover

Place the chicken in a large casserole with the onions, carrots and leeks chopped roughly and the spices and orange peel. Add cold water to come halfway up the chicken. Cover well. Place on a moderate heat and simmer for 1–1½ hours until the chicken is cooked. It will have no brown colour. The chicken is removed and kept warm and a little of the broth thickened with flour to make a sauce. Carve the chicken, smothered in the sauce. The vegetables can be served alongside or added to the remainder of the broth to make a soup with the addition of vermicelli and served with chopped parsley. Any remaining leftover chicken can be used for the following fricassee recipe.

White fricassee

A fricassee is meat cut into small pieces or slices, cooked in a thick sauce in a shallow pan. It is often a white meat (but sometimes lamb) and the result is often (but not always) a white dish, as it is in Sarah Longe's recipe overleaf.

Fricassée is a French word which came into use in the fifteenth century. Its exact origin is far from clear, though the concept of frying – the shallow pan – seems to have something to do with it. The word reached English and the recipe became popular in England in the mid-sixteenth century: it was quite a new thing in Shakespeare's time, and Mrs Longe's recipe is almost the earliest known.

A white ffrigasy. Take the flesh of 6 chickens and cut the legs and wings into pieces, and the other cut in as broad thin pieces as you can; then take strong broth, and a bundle of sweet herbs, and large mace, and boil all together till they be tender; then put your chicken into the pan, then take 9 yolks of eggs, and beat them with a little white wine, or a little vinegar, a little sugar, and the juice of a lemon, but fry your chickens; when they are ready then put in your eggs and toss them well together, fry them not too long after your eggs be in, for they will curdle; so serve them with sippets; strew minced parsley over the dish.

Mrs. Sarah Longe her Receipt Booke (c. 1610)

Chicken fricassee

300 g/10 oz cooked chicken in morsels
Salt and pepper
Pinch of ground mace
1 egg yolk
1 tablespoon cream
45 g/1^1/$_2$ oz butter
45 g/1^1/$_2$ oz plain flour
250 ml/8^1/$_2$ fl oz/1 cup chicken stock
100 ml/3^1/$_2$ fl oz/^{1}/$_2$ cup milk

In a pan melt the butter and add the flour to make a roux. Season with salt, pepper and mace. Gradually stir in the stock and milk until the sauce has thickened. Add the cooked chicken and warm through in the sauce. Just before serving stir in the cream and egg yolk. Serve the fricassee on croûtes of toasted bread.

Farts of Portingale

Portingale (to get that word out of the way first) is Portugal. We have two contemporary recipes for farts of Portingale. The earliest, from the 1584/1591 *Book of Cookrye*, is for a sweet version of the dish, and is not quoted here because it is not sufficiently explicit. Instead we choose the 1594 recipe in *The*

Good Huswifes Handmaide for the Kitchin, which is savoury, based on minced lamb and cooked in beef broth. This is followed in the same cookbook by a sweet version called 'fists of Portingale'. As we can see, fists are bigger than farts – as big as tennis balls in fact – but this second recipe could easily be varied to make small, sweet farts of Portingale as incompletely described in the *Book of Cookrye*.

How to make Farts of Portingale. Take a piece of a leg of mutton, mince it small and season it with cloves, mace, pepper and salt, and dates minced with currants: then roll it into round rolls, and so into little balls, and so boil them in a little beef broth and so serve them forth.

How to make Fystes of Portingale. Take some sweet suet minced small, the yolks of two eggs, with grated bread and currants: temper all these together with a litle saffron, cinnamon, ginger, and a little salt: then seethe them in a little bastard or sack a little while: and when they have boiled a little take it up, and cast some sugar to it, and so make balls of it as big as tennis balls, and lay four or five in a dish, and pour on some of the broth that they were sodden in, and so serve them.

The Good Huswifes Handmaide for the Kitchin (1594)

Farts of Portingale

250 g/9 oz minced lamb
1 teaspoon ground mace
Salt
Chopped dried fruit to taste (e.g. sultanas, apricots or prunes)
Handful of coarse breadcrumbs
1 egg

Mix all the ingredients and bind together with the egg. Form into small balls with the hands. Poach gently in a little stock, or fry if preferred. Serve in the broth. We have sometimes made them with redcurrant jelly added to the broth before serving. Alternatively, with less attention to history, serve with chutneys of your choice. They would also be tasty served cold with a yoghurt and mint dressing.

Boiled stockfish

Cod was not a familiar fish in medieval England: at least, not under that name. In Shakespeare's plays there is only one mention of 'cod' as the name of a fish, and that one is highly ambiguous (Iago, in *Othello*, is sniping at women who 'change the cod's head for the salmon's tail'). In early English writings 'cod' nearly always means a pea or bean pod, or a bag, or the scrotum; hence the term 'codpiece' for an item of apparel that covered and drew discreet attention to a man's sexual parts.

The English knew of the fish that we call cod, but in its dried form, which was called 'stockfish'. Few had ever tasted it fresh: otherwise Thomas Cogan could hardly have written, as he does:

[Stockfish] is in taste fresh, yet brought to us dried from Iceland and other countries northward. Concerning which fish I will say no more than Erasmus hath written in his Colloquio: Est genus piscis quod vocatur Anglice stockfish: non magis nutrit quam lignum. Yet I have eaten of a pie made only with stockfish, which hath been very good, but the goodness was not so much in the fish as in the cookery . . . Therefore a good cook is a good jewel and to be made much of.

The last assertion is of course true. The first statement, that stockfish 'is in taste fresh', few nowadays would accept, which is exactly why stockfish, though still produced in the old-fashioned way, has gone out of fashion nearly everywhere; but stockfish is not salty, and that is certainly the reason for Cogan's claim. Stockfish, air-dried and with all possible moisture expelled, is as hard as wood, as the Latin quotation from Erasmus hints: 'There is a kind of fish called stockfish in English: it is no better food than wood.'

Stockfish, fished in north Atlantic waters and dried in Iceland and Norway before export, was to be replaced in the seventeenth century by a different product from the newly discovered Grand Banks off Newfoundland. In the climate of Newfoundland and Nova Scotia cod could not be air-dried; instead it was salted, and plentiful salt cod captured the market. Much later still, fresh cod was to become a popular item of the British diet. Now the era of cheap cod in any form may be over.

A kitchen scene with a cook preparing fish and a lobster. Print after Pieter Aertsen, from a series by Jacob Matham published in Haarlem in 1603. Engraving, 24.5 x 32.8 cm. British Museum, PD 1857,0613.524.

To seeth stocke fish. Take stockfish and water it well, and then put out all the baste from the fish, then put it into a pipkin, and put in no more water than shall cover it, then set it on the fire, and as soon as it beginneth to boil on the one side, then turn the other side to the fire, and as soon as it beginneth to boil on the other side, take it off and put it into a colander, and let the water run out from it, but put in salt in the boiling of it, then take a little fair water and sweet butter, and let it boil in a dish until it be something thick, then pour it on the stockfish, and so serve it in.

The Good Huswifes Handmaide for the Kitchin (1594)

Stockfish

Estocaficada, a speciality of Nice whose main ingredient is stockfish, is still made today. Jacques Médecin in *Cuisine Niçoise* explains a less orthodox method of preparing stockfish, using 100 g/3½ oz unsoaked stockfish, 4 cloves garlic, black pepper and olive oil. The stockfish is beaten against a rock with a hammer and reduced to a paste; this can instead be done with a pestle and mortar and the garlic incorporated at the same time. For those who can't get stockfish or prefer to use fresh cod or haddock, this too can easily be reduced to a paste, adding the garlic, perhaps a little salt, perhaps a little verjuice or vinegar. Whatever the fish being used, heat olive oil in a frying pan, add the pounded mixture and brown gently. Serve spread on brown bread. Lemon juice can be squeezed over if wished, replacing the vinegar or verjuice.

Apple fritters

Crab-apples are a native English fruit. Cultivated apples, though they seem very much at home in England, are not: they were introduced by the Romans, and they stayed on when the Romans departed. If any fruit is typical of England it is the apple, though its nutritional reputation has been, to say the least, equivocal. Early English writers on nutrition, like their Greek and Roman predecessors, advised keeping apples as long as possible and preferably roasting or otherwise cooking them. Fresh apples were not only dangerous to the stomach with their raw juices; Thomas Cogan says they were also:

. . . thought to quench the flame of Venus, according to that old English saying, 'He that will not a wife wed, Must eat a cold apple when he goeth to bed'.

'The bigness of a groat' in the recipe below comes out as not more than an inch across (a groat was a silver coin worth four pence). Which seems unexpectedly small, but the apples to be used might be semi-dried with concentrated flavour.

Instead of simple sugar it is possible to use blanch powder, a medieval delicacy still popular in the early seventeenth century, as a garnish.

To make frittors with apples. Take fine flour, and temper it with butter and a little salt, and make a batter, and take a very little saffron to colour your batter withal, and when your batter is made, strain it through a strainer, then cut your apples of the bigness of a groat, and put them to your batter; then put your suet to the fire, and when it is hot, put a piece of your apples to your suet, and if it rise quickly, then your stuff is well seasoned, if it abide in the bottom, then it is not half enough: therefore when it riseth from the bottom, fill your pan one after another as fast as ye can, and when they are fair coloured, take them out with a scummer, and put them in a platter, and always while they are in the pan stir them with a stick, and look that ye have liquor enough. Then take your fritters, and put them in a fair platter, and then scrape sugar enough upon them.

The Good Huswifes Handmaide for the Kitchin (1594)

Apples on a branch. Drawing from an album by Jacques Le Moyne. *c.* 1585. Watercolour and bodycolour, 21.4 x 14.1 cm. British Museum, PD 1962,0714.1.40, purchased with assistance from the Pilgrim Trust and the Art Fund.

[Blanch powder.] With two ounces of sugar, a quarter of an ounce of ginger, and half a quarter of an ounce of cinnamon, all beaten small into powder, you may make a very good blanch powder to strow upon roasted apples, quinces or wardens, or to sauce a hen.

Thomas Cogan, *The Haven of Health* (1636)

Grimole

Apple fritters are made in a similar manner today, and the use of ale in batter mixture is still well known. If one prefers to avoid deep frying then the French *grimole*, a cross between a *clafoutis* and a pancake, is a suitable substitute. In past times *grimole* was cooked in a bread oven, in a cabbage leaf which served the purpose of a mould (and gave a distinctive flavour which not everyone might like today).

125 g/4 oz plain flour
1 teaspoon baking powder
Pinch of salt
100 g/3¹/₂ oz caster sugar
2 eggs
3 tablespoons vegetable oil
125 ml/4 fl oz/¹/₂ cup milk
4 dessert apples, peeled and sliced

Preheat the oven to 190°C/375°F/gas mark 5. Make a batter with the flour, sugar, baking powder, salt, eggs and oil. Gradually whisk in the milk until you have a thick batter. Tip in the apples and pour into a greased mould – the shallower the better – a 30-cm/12-inch flan dish would suit. Cook for about 45 minutes. Dredge with sugar and serve hot with cream.

The House of
Feasting (detail).
Print after Maerten
de Vos, from a
series by Nicolaas
de Bruyn, published
c. 1600. Engraving,
32.5 x 38.8 cm.
British Museum,
PD 1928,0313.184.

'I am a great eater of beef'

TWELFTH NIGHT

About two years intervene between the *Henry IV* plays and *Twelfth Night*, which was complete in early 1602. During those two years the Lord Chamberlain's Servants built the Globe Theatre; during those same two years Shakespeare came into his own. On the handy quarto editions of the company's older plays he is sometimes credited as writer, sometimes as reviser, and sometimes not named at all: that's the case with *Romeo and Juliet*, often reprinted but never credited to Shakespeare until his collected works were published in the First Folio, in 1623, seven years after his death.

On any new play that Shakespeare wrote after 1601 and that appeared in print, 'by William Shakespeare' is blazoned on the title page. But that doesn't apply to all his work. *Twelfth Night* itself, for example, was little known and never printed at all until its appearance in the First Folio. Its first known performance was at a private celebration of Candlemas Day (2 February 1602), when John Manningham, law student at the Middle Temple in London, noted in his diary:

At our feast we had a play called Twelve Night, or What You Will, much like The Comedy of Errors or Menaechmi in Plautus, but most like and near to that in Italian called Inganni. A good practice in it [is] to make the steward believe his lady-widow was in love with him . . .

Manningham had done his homework. This new comedy was indirectly based on the Italian play *Gl'ingannati* ('The Deceived'), written for performance at the Siena carnival in 1532 and popular enough to have been translated into French and Latin before Shakespeare set to work on it. The Latin version *Laelia* had been put on by the students of Queen's College, Cambridge, in 1595. Shakespeare, however, worked from an English retelling, and he turns the story into a comedy of humours. He changes the names, changes the setting, and produces a romance set in Illyria, a strange country, some of whose inhabitants have names such as Malvolio and Viola while others include the broadly comic Sir Toby Belch and the straight man Sir Andrew Aguecheek.

'Does not our life consist of the four elements?' Toby demands. 'Faith, so they say', Andrew replies seriously, 'but I think it rather consists of eating and drinking.' 'Thou'rt a scholar! Let us therefore eat and drink. Maria, I say! a stoup of wine!' Sir Andrew is fated to be snubbed (but Toby always knows how to revive him: 'O knight, thou lack'st a cup of canary') and is nervous about his diet. He is not alone among Renaissance hypochondriacs in regularly worrying that beef makes one dull – and regularly dismissing the thought just before each meal –

'But I am a great eater of beef, and I believe that does harm to my wit.'
'No question.'
'An I thought that, I'd forswear it.'

At this point in *Twelfth Night* we are certainly in England, not Illyria. It was the English, then as now, who were famous in Europe for their beef-eating, to say nothing of their dullness, to say nothing of their illogicality. The law students of the Middle Temple were ready to laugh at these thoughts even if the audience at the Globe was not.

We are in England, without a doubt. The fantasy Illyrian household, where Sir Toby can always get a stoup of wine if he flirts with Olivia's housekeeper, is not so very far away from the Pages' household in *The Merry Wives of Windsor* (written, quite possibly, in the same year as *Twelfth Night*), in which Falstaff flirts with Mistress Page and makes a fool of himself. In this Windsor household we know at least part of the dinner menu to which the broadly comic Falstaff and the straight man Slender are invited. 'Come', George Page insists, 'we have a hot venison pasty to dinner. Come gentlemen, I hope we shall drink down all unkindness.' We know the dessert too: 'I will make an end of my dinner; there's pippins and cheese to come.' The pippins are another kind of apple, best eaten crisp and fresh. In the evening there will be further nourishment: 'Yet be cheerful, knight! Thou shalt eat a posset to-night at my house.' But how will he take his posset? 'With eggs, sir?' 'Simple of itself; I'll no pullet-sperm in my brewage.'

Merry Wives, with its firmly English setting, has room for jibes at typical foreign food and drink, Flemish, Welsh and Irish: 'I will rather trust a Fleming with my butter, Parson Hugh the Welshman with my cheese, an Irishman with my aquavitae bottle.' There is talk of metheglin, the spiced mead of Wales. Food is a recurrent theme in Falstaff's conversation: 'The world's mine oyster, which I with sword will open', he blusters; and 'Revenged I will be, as sure as his guts are made of puddings'; and again, 'Have I lived to be carried in a basket, and to be thrown in the Thames like a barrow of butcher's offal? Well, if I be served such another trick, I'll have my brains ta'en out and buttered!'

Published in 1602 and frequently performed (at least once at court at Queen Elizabeth's command), *Merry Wives* became a perennial favourite. Set at Windsor and reviving the long-dead Falstaff and his crew, it showed countrymen as Londoners saw them and Londoners as they saw themselves.

Knife and fork with gold-mounted agate handles. ?German, c. 1600.
L. (knife) 22.4 cm, (fork) 20.2 cm. British Museum, P&E WB.206,
bequeathed by Baron Ferdinand Anselm de Rothschild.

Roast rib of beef with pepper and vinegar sauce

Beef was regarded, not only abroad but by many in England too, as the English national food. The clichés and assumptions that came with the word 'beef' were quite complex, however. There was a widespread opinion (not quite forgotten even today) that certain foods, locally produced and commonly eaten, were in some way ideal for the people who ate them. Hence in Shakespeare's historical plays French soldiers, preparing to fight the English, talk of the beef their opponents eat to make them big and fierce and stupid (in *Henry V*), and of the 'fat bull beeves' the English can't get and how weak they are as a consequence (in *Henry VI part 1*).

Roasting beef was the classic way to present it, though boiled beef may well have been a more familiar dish, week in, week out.

A dubble rib of beef rosted, sauce pepper and vinagre.

A Book of Cookrye (1591)

Roast rib of beef

Rub the joint well with a little olive oil or dripping and season with salt and pepper. Then cook, in a preheated oven, as follows: for a joint of up to 2 kg/4½ lb, roast in the oven for 20 minutes at 210°C/410°F/gas mark 6; for a larger joint up to 3 kg/7 lb, roast for 30 minutes at 210°C/410°F/gas mark 6; then in all cases continue to roast for 30 minutes per kg at 160°C/325°C/gas mark 3. Cooking time will vary if you like your beef pink or if you want it well done.

It is important to remove the joint half an hour in advance of eating time and leave to rest. The pan can be deglazed with red wine before the gravy is made. Beef can be served with mustard (on Tewkesbury mustard see page 18) as a condiment.

Interior of a kitchen. Print by David Teniers the Younger, c. 1625–90. Etching, 15.3 x 20 cm.
British Museum, PD S.6766.

Hodgepot

The word hodgepot doesn't quite occur in a Shakespeare play, but it's there behind the scenes when Ford in *The Merry Wives of Windsor* calls Falstaff 'a hodge-pudding – a bag of flax!' This certainly compares the fat knight to a typical hodgepot, a meaty, greasy stew.

The word and the idea had been around in England for three centuries already, having apparently crossed the Channel from France, where *hochepot* can be analysed, by the enthusiastic word historian, into 'shake-the-pot'. You shake the pot so that things won't stick to it; why you don't stir it is not explained. Those who don't believe this can look to Holland, where words such as *hutspot* are equally familiar.

In sixteenth-century England the word has not settled into any fixed shape. We find *hotchpot*, *hodgepot*, *hotchpotch*, *hodgepodge*, all with the same meaning. It is a dish of high status: not long after Shakespeare's time *The Closet of Sir Kenelm Digby Opened* includes a recipe for 'The Queen Mother's hotchpot of mutton'. The Queen Mother concerned is Henriette-Marie, mother of Charles II, daughter of Henry IV of France and Maria de' Medici. Where she got her taste for hotchpot we don't know, but there is a contemporary recipe by the courtly chef Lancelot de Casteau, who worked in Flanders, for a hodgepot of veal (*heuspot de veau*).

These four spellings continue to be used until the late nineteenth century: at which point, rather suddenly, the new form *hot-pot* appears – and becomes the name of a typical Lancashire dish – while the surviving old form *hotchpotch* drops its culinary meaning and turns into a general mixture or unplanned mess.

Marigold flowers (*Calendula officinalis*) are called for in the following recipe. Still familiar in English gardens, they are no longer familiar in the kitchen. They added colour – saffron will serve as a substitute here – and also medicinal virtues. Henry Lyte, in his translation of the Dutch *New Herbal*, wrote that 'the conserve that is made of the flowers of marigolds, taken in the morning fasting, cureth the trembling and shaking of the heart; it is also good to be used against the plague and corruption of the air'.

To make a Hodgepodge. Boil a neck of mutton or a fat rump of beef, and when it is well boiled, take the best of the broth and put it into a pipkin and put a good many onions to it, two handful of marigold flowers, and a handful of parsley fine-picked and gross-shred and not too small, and so boil them in the broth and thick it with strained bread, putting therein gross-beaten pepper and a spoonful of vinegar, and let it boil somewhat thick, and so lay it upon your meat.

A Book of Cookrye (1591); an identical recipe is in *The Good Huswifes Handmaide for the Kitchin* (1594)

Hodgepot

This recipe creates a dilemma: what to substitute for the marigold flowers, not available in many kitchens? They added colour and health benefits rather than flavour; therefore saffron, as listed here, would approach the required effect. So would turmeric, but this spice was not known in Elizabethan kitchens.

500 g/1 lb 2 oz stewing steak
4 rashers streaky bacon
3 large onions
3 carrots
750 ml/1^1/$_4$ pints/3 cups water
Handful of coarsely chopped parsley
Salt and pepper
1 tablespoon verjuice
Flour to thicken
^{1}/$_2$ teaspoon saffron

Prepare and chop the vegetables and put in a casserole dish with the chopped bacon, seasoning and parsley. Place the meat on top; add the water and verjuice. Cover with greaseproof paper and put on a lid. Cook in the oven at 180°C/350°F/gas mark 4 for 30 minutes, then reduce the heat to 140°C/275°F/gas mark 1 for at least 2 hours or until the meat is cooked. Take out of the oven and remove the beef. Mix the flour and saffron together and blend to a paste with 2 tablespoons of juice from the casserole. Mix into the casserole on a gentle heat and stir until the juice thickens.

Serve the meat with the thickened sauce and the vegetables.

A cake

A cake, to Shakespeare, was a concept that overlapped with the modern English cake but didn't coincide with it. We need to know this before trying to make sense of Toby Belch's remark to the censorious Malvolio: 'Art any more than a steward? Dost thou think, because thou art virtuous, that there shall be no more cakes and ale?' Malvolio is only a steward after all, and whatever postures he assumes, life will go on. The world will not be turned off its course, and people will go to taverns and enjoy their 'cakes and ale'. Ale was the typical everyday drink, and cakes were what you ate while enjoying your ale: hard cakes, oat cakes possibly, not so very far off from being biscuits (that, certainly, is the texture of the sugar cakes in the next recipe).

As for their flavourings, cakes could be sweet or savoury, and they were quite likely to be loaf-shaped. This is the exact sense of the word *cake* (yes, *cake*, not *gâteau*) when it is used in modern French. Imagine tea loaf, give a thought to olive bread, consider waffles; these are all cakes in the Shakespearean sense of the word. A waffle is accurately described in a French–English dictionary of that period as a 'cake of fyne floure made in a print of yron'. Where we might have expected 'unleavened bread', the King James Bible version of the Exodus story gives us 'unleavened cakes'.

Caraway comfits, called for in the following recipe, are tiny sweets made of single caraway seeds coated in sugar: see the introduction, page 18.

To make a cake. Take half a bushel of flour, 8 pound of currants, and 5 pound of butter, and boil it by itself, and skim it, 3 pints of cream, and boil it, 3 quarters of a pound of sugar, one ounce of mace, one ounce of nutmegs, half an ounce of cinnamon, a little ginger, half a quarter of a pint of rose water, two eggs (half the whites) and half a pound of caraway comfits, one quart of yeast, and let it stand in the oven an hour and a half.

Note. Make 3 holes in the flour, and put the eggs in one hole, the melted butter in the other, and the yeast in the 3rd, and have a care that you scald not the yeast with the cream when you mingle the cake.

Mrs. Sarah Longe her Receipt Booke (c. 1610)

Barm brack

Barm brack, an Irish fruit bread, makes a good equivalent for an early seventeenth-century cake.

450 g/1 lb risen white bread dough
75 g/3 oz caster sugar
75 g/3 oz lard
2 eggs
100 g/3 1/2 oz currants or raisins
1/2 teaspoon each ground ginger, nutmeg and cinnamon

Mix the spices with the sugar. Work the lard and the sugar mixture into the dough and knead in the beaten eggs and finally the dried fruit. Knead until well blended. Shape to fit a greased 900 g/2 lb loaf tin.

Cover with clingfilm and leave to prove for 45 minutes. Bake in a hot oven at 220°C/425°F/gas mark 7 for 30 minutes. Reduce the heat to 180°C/350°F/gas mark 4 and continue to bake for a further 30 minutes. Cool and serve.

Sugar cakes

Cakes differed from bread not necessarily because they were sweet, but because they often included spices and other such strong and health-giving flavourings. There were rose-cakes, laden with rose water. There were tansy-cakes flavoured and coloured with costmary. And among all these other possibilities there were sugar cakes, flavoured with the valuable crystalline spice that came from the Mediterranean islands – not yet from the West Indies – and was so nourishing and strengthening to the feeble Elizabethan constitution. If it tasted good, that was merely an added benefit.

The process of sugar manufacture. Print from a series after Jan van der Straet, published in Antwerp *c.* 1580–1605. Engraving, 20.8 x 27.4 cm. British Museum, PD 1948,0410.4.203, bequeathed by Sir Hans Sloane.

The strong, enticing flavour of sugar was a good way to conceal other less welcome ingredients, as suggested by Nicholas Breton's poem *Pasquil's Fool's-cap* published in 1600:

Such vile conjunctions such constructions make
That some are poisoned with a sugar cake.

The moral? Keep on good terms with the cook.

To make sugar cakes. Take a pound of butter, and wash it in rosewater, and half a pound of sugar, and half a dozen spoonfuls of thick cream, and the yolks of 4 eggs, and a little mace finely beaten, and as much fine flour as it will wet, and work it well together; then roll them out very thin, and cut them with a glass, and prick them very thick with a great pin, and lay them on plates, and so bake them gently.

Mrs. Sarah Longe her Receipt Booke (c. 1610)

Shrewsbury biscuits

100 g/3¹/₂ oz butter
225 g/8 oz plain flour
110 g/4 oz caster sugar
Pinch of salt
¹/₂ teaspoon each ground cinnamon and nutmeg
2 teaspoons caraway seeds
1 egg
1 teaspoon rose water (or, if preferred, water)

Rub the butter into the flour, sugar and spices (except the caraway) until the mixture resembles breadcrumbs. Now add the caraway seeds. Beat the egg and a few drops of the rose water and use to bind the dry ingredients to form a dough. Water may be added if too dry. Roll out until about 5 mm thick. Cut out the cakes using a 10-cm/4-inch cutter. Bake on a greased baking tray at 180°C/350°F/gas mark 4 for about 20 minutes or until golden brown. Dredge with sugar while still warm.

Posset

A posset is a very ancient concept – almost as old as cheese, perhaps, because the distinctive feature of posset is that it is curdled, much as cheese curdles, though by the action of a different range of additives. Posset, as known by this name since medieval times, is a milk drink curdled by the action of an acid drink such as wine, ale or nowadays fruit juice. The word is not found in other languages and its origin is unknown.

If the whey was separated from the curds as a posset was being made, the result was a 'posset curd', as in the recipe quoted below, and this would certainly be thick enough to eat rather than drink. So it is in one of the two cases in which posset is mentioned in Shakespeare's plays: in *The Merry Wives of Windsor* George Page invites Sir John Falstaff to 'eat a posset tonight at my house'. In the other case, in *Macbeth*, we aren't told whether the posset was eaten or drunk. The resourceful Lady Macbeth simply says: 'The surfeited grooms do mock their charge with snores. I have drugged their possets.' From these two cases together we can see that a posset was a late-night drink, though not always such an effective sleeping-draught as Lady Macbeth describes.

If the whey was not separated there was all the more need for a posset cup, a familiar item of Elizabethan household equipment which might be equally useful in drinking a modern milkshake: there, too, the drinker likes to choose how much of the liquid, and how much of the solid, to take in each mouthful. Posset cups were typically made of wood, like trenchers. 'He is a most excellent turner, and will turn you wassail-bowls and posset cups', says a character in the anonymous 1606 play *Sir Giles Goosecap*. A wassail-bowl, containing spiced ale or wine, would be passed around the group of drinkers at a Christmas or New Year's Eve celebration.

To make a good posset curd. Take your milk and set it on the fire, and let it seethe, put in your yolks of eggs according to the quantity of your milk. But see that your eggs be tempered with some of the milk ere ye put them to the milk that is on the fire, or else it will fall together and mar all, and ye must stir it still till it seethe and begin to rise. Then take it off the fire, but before ye take it off, have your drink ready in a fair basin, on a chafing dish of coals, and pour the milk into the basin as it standeth over the chafing dish with fire, so cover it, and let it stand a while. Then take it up and cast on cinnamon and sugar, and so serve it in.

The Good Huswifes Handmaide for the Kitchin (1594)

Lemon posset

400 ml/14 fl oz/1³/₄ cups double cream
125 ml/4 fl oz/¹/₂ cup caster sugar
125 ml/4 fl oz/¹/₂ cup lemon juice
Grated zest of 1 lemon

The name posset persists for this refreshing drink but the typical sweet wine of early recipes has given way to lemon juice.

Heat the cream and sugar over a gentle heat until it comes to the boil. Simmer for 3 minutes. Take off the heat and whisk in the lemon juice and zest. Leave to rest for 2 to 3 minutes and then pour into 4 glass dishes or wine glasses. Leave to cool then cover with clingfilm and refrigerate until set. Shrewsbury biscuits (see recipe on page 73) are ideal to serve alongside lemon posset.

Tin-glazed earthenware posset pot. Made in Southwark, London, in 1632. H. (including lid) 21 cm. British Museum, P&E 1887,0307,E.101, given by Sir Augustus Wollaston Franks.

The wedding feast
in Cana in Galilee
(detail). Print by
Odoardo Fialetti,
1600–38. Etching,
36 x 43.5 cm.
British Museum,
PD W,9.103.

'The funeral baked meats'

HAMLET

At the Danish court Hamlet, the late king's son, is astonished to meet his friend Horatio who he thought was still at university in Wittenberg. Horatio explains:

'My lord, I came to see your father's funeral.'
'I prithee do not mock me, fellow-student.
I think it was to see my mother's wedding.'

Horatio picks up the irony in Hamlet's words and is forced to agree:

'Indeed, my lord, it followed hard upon.'
'Thrift, thrift, Horatio. The funeral baked meats
Did coldly furnish forth the marriage tables.'

These last sarcastic lines are all that Hamlet needs to say – and all that the play tells us – of old Hamlet's funeral dinner and of the

feast at which his brother and successor Claudius hastily married his widow Gertrude. What more was wanted? This is scene-setting: the real story of *Hamlet* is Hamlet's discovery that his uncle Claudius was his father's murderer, and how he then avenges the murder.

Alexandre Dumas's French translation of *Hamlet*, a theatrical success in 1847, skips the opening scene on the battlements and begins royally with the council at which Claudius recounts his succession and marriage. The meeting between Hamlet and Horatio soon follows, and Hamlet's sarcasm comes over well in French:

> . . . Calcul de ménagère!
> Les restes refroidis du funèbre repas
> Au banquet nuptial ont pu fournir des plats.

When the Dumas version was turned into an even more successful opera by Ambroise Thomas, the librettist decided that these few lines of understated bitter humour between fellow students were not enough. They are dropped. A full two months are now said to elapse from old Hamlet's death to Gertrude's wedding breakfast: the funeral baked meats, *les restes refroidis*, would have been cold indeed. The opera's opening scene is the very feast at which Claudius marries Gertrude and crowns her his consort, queen of Denmark for the second time. The climax is less tragic in one important detail: Hamlet survives.

Thus, in its nineteenth-century operatic incarnation, the Hamlet story begins with a wedding feast. Strangely, in its most primitive version, a story known to Shakespeare but rejected by him, the story ends with a funeral feast, a scene of violence even bloodier than the last act of Shakespeare's *Hamlet*.

Shakespeare's play *The Tragicall Historie of Hamlet, Prince of Denmarke* was first printed in 1603. He may have worked from a popular recent play on the Hamlet theme, from a French retelling of the story, and perhaps from other books too, but the underlying source of all of these was in any case the twelfth-century Danish history by Saxo Grammaticus, *Gesta Danorum*. Saxo based his narrative on even older legends. In those early versions Claudius, Gertrude, Polonius, Ophelia, Rosencrantz and Guildenstern can all be recognized, though not under these names, and the tragedy has a quite different climax. Hamlet is sent to England and returns in time to find the Danish court celebrating his own funeral feast. Pretending to be a fool, he joins the waiters handing out wine to the guests. When all are dead drunk he cuts down the tapestries and hangings that his mother had woven, trapping them in the folds, and sets fire to the hall. All are burned to ashes. Meanwhile he finds his uncle's apartment, wakes him with the unwelcome news that Hamlet has returned, and kills him as he struggles to rise. The story has resemblances to some others in Norse and Icelandic legend, that of 'Burnt Njal' for example, but it is not Shakespearean. We can agree with Shakespeare on that.

So Gertrude and Claudius's wedding feast is only hinted at in *Hamlet*: the audience must take it as read. There is one Shakespeare play in which a wedding banquet is played on stage, and that is *The Taming of the Shrew*. Here too, unluckily for the cook, the playwright doesn't focus on the food: the point is the byplay among the newly married couples, in the course of which Petruchio is able to prove, to everyone's surprise, that he has 'tamed' his 'shrew' – or, to put it another way, that he and Kate have sorted things out better and faster than their competitors.

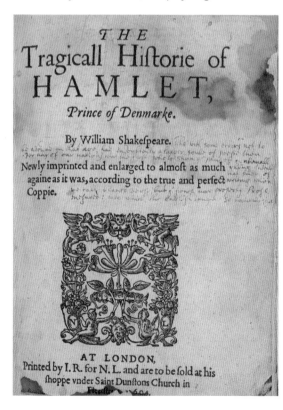

The tragicall historie of Hamlet, Prince of Denmarke by William Shakespeare. Title page to *Hamlet*, Second Quarto, 1604. Folger Shakespeare Library.

Coffins

The one item on the wedding feast menu that Shakespeare himself gives us in *Hamlet* is the 'baked meats'. These are certainly pies, the kind of well-built pies that conserve their contents and can be eaten hot or cold. It would indeed have been a frugal idea to reuse them, cold, at the wedding feast (if it really followed within a few days).

Are they meat pies? What we call meat was not necessarily in Hamlet's or Shakespeare's mind: *meat* in early seventeenth-century English could mean food in general, and so *baked meats* really means pies and fancy baked goods in general. This is what the term means when, just eight years after *Hamlet* first appeared in print, it is used in the King James version of the book of Genesis. The chief baker tells Joseph his dream:

I had three white baskets on my head: and in the uppermost basket there was of all manner of bakemeats for Pharaoh; and the birds did eat them out of the basket.

A pastry pie case, built up solidly empty and prebaked before being filled with the pie's eventual contents, was properly known as a coffin. A 'custard-coffin' – a custard pie without the custard – is what Petruchio in *The Taming of the Shrew* calls a hat. This is a hat that he decides, for tactical purposes and to test Kate's resolve, that he does not like just now. In using the word Petruchio is not hinting at death and funerals: a coffin could, at this period, be a wooden box rather than a pie-case, but it was not usually a box for placing a dead body in.

To make paste, and to raise coffins. Take fine flour, and lay it on a board, and take a certain of yolks of eggs as your quantity of flour is, then take a certain of butter and water, and boil them together, but ye must take heed ye put not too many yolks of eggs, for if you do, it will make it dry and not pleasant in eating: and ye must take heed ye put not in too much butter, for if you do, it will make it so fine and so short that you cannot raise. And this paste is good to raise all manner of coffins: likewise if ye bake venison, bake it in the paste above named.

The Good Huswifes Handmaide for the Kitchin (1594)

Hot water crust pastry

The paste recipe of 1594 involves boiling the water and fat, as with a modern hot water crust pastry, although lard is used instead of butter. If hot water crust pastry is too time-consuming or difficult one could instead make shortcrust pastry, and I have given both alternatives below. I personally prefer shortcrust pastry for small pies: it's easier to work.

300 g / 10 oz plain white flour
Pinch of salt
Pinch of ground mace
60 g / 2 oz lard or white vegetable fat
150 ml / 5 fl oz / ²/₃ cup water

Sift the flour, salt and mace into a bowl and form a well in the middle. Heat the fat and water in a pan until the fat melts, increase the heat and bring to the boil. Pour the liquid into the well and incorporate the flour. Beat together. Knead gently in the bowl until smooth: do not overwork as it will become tough. Cover in a warm tea towel. Use the pastry while it is still warm.

Shortcrust pastry

225 g / 8 oz plain white flour
Pinch of salt
¹/₂ teaspoon ground mace
110 g / 4 oz butter, or 55 g / 2 oz butter and 55 g / 2 oz lard or white vegetable fat
45–60 ml / 3–4 tablespoons water

Sift the flour, salt and mace into a bowl and add the fat, cut into small pieces. Rub the fat into the flour until the mixture resembles fine breadcrumbs. Add the water gradually and blend with a knife until the mixture binds. Use hands to collect the dough to a smooth ball. Leave to rest in clingfilm in a fridge for half an hour before using.

Chewets

This paste (page 80) was used to make chewets, small pasties containing various meats or fish. Meat chewets also contained dried fruits and spices. A sixteenth-century ballad attacking the clergy, *The Image of Hypocrisy*, talks of cardinals who:

. . . wallow bestially
As hogs do in a sty,
Serving their god, their belly
With chewets and with jelly,
With venison and with tarts
And portingale farts
To ease their holy hearts.

They were good and luxurious little pasties, then – ideal finger food for any banquets, including the ones at which cardinals wallowed bestially – but they aren't mentioned, as such, in any Shakespeare play; except that, like so many other self-indulgent varieties of food, they turn up in the conversation surrounding Sir John Falstaff. In *Henry IV part 1*, interrupting the tense discussion in which Worcester has just denied looking for rebellion, Falstaff butts in with a humorous explanation: 'Rebellion lay in his way, and he found it!' Prince Hal may not be displeased at this broad hint that Worcester is merely playing with words; but he gently hushes his old friend, 'Peace, chewet, peace!' The meaning here is disputed, but Sir John was indeed a mixture of meat, fruit and spices stuffed into a case – a chewet.

Pewter cup. Made in London, c. 1600. H. 14.8 cm.
British Museum, P&E 1980,0502.1.

To make chewites of veale. Take a leg of veal and parboil it, then mince it with beef suet, take almost as much of your suet as of your veal, and take a good quantity of ginger, and a little saffron to colour it. Take half a goblet of white wine, and two or three good handful of grapes, and put them all together with salt, and so put them in coffins, and let them boil a quarter of an hour.

The Good Huswifes Handmaide for the Kitchin (1594)

Chewets

Chewets can be made using many combinations of minced cooked meat and fruit – chicken and cranberries, pork and apple, lamb and apricot, etc. It is possible to use ready-made rillettes (potted meat) as the meat in the mixture: duck rillettes with orange (Elizabethans liked the flavour of orange with meat, see page 34) or goose rillettes with grated lemon zest. Chewets are among the ancestors of modern mince pies.

300 g/10 oz cooked meat, e.g. veal
50 g/2 oz suet
1 teaspoon ground ginger
Pinch of saffron
1/2 glass white wine
6 dried apricots
Pinch of salt
1 quantity of hot water crust pastry, or shortcrust pastry (see page 81)
1 egg to glaze

Soak the apricots in the wine. Mince the cooked veal and mix well with the suet, ginger, saffron and salt. Chop the soaked apricots into small pieces and mix into the other ingredients with enough wine to blend.

Roll out the pastry to line 10 bun compartments of a baking tray. Fill the pies and cover with pastry. Seal the edges, make an air hole in the top and glaze with beaten egg.

Bake in a preheated oven, 200°C/400°F/gas mark 6, for 15 minutes, then reduce the heat to 180°C/350°F/gas mark 4 for a further 30 minutes or until nicely brown. If using shortcrust pastry, simply cook at 190°C/375°F/gas mark 5 for 20–25 minutes.

Florentine

A Florentine, still known by this name in Scotland as late as the nineteenth century, was the kind of pie that is familiar today in which a baking dish is lined with a thinner layer of uncooked pastry, the pie filling is added, a pastry top goes on last, and the whole is baked. Within this general type, a Florentine was usually filled with veal, to which dates, raisins and various spices were added. In the recipe quoted here 'hard-sod' means hard-boiled (sod is the old past participle of seethe).

To make a florentine. Take veal, and some of the kidney of the loin, or cold veal roasted, cold capon or pheasant, which of them you will, and mince it very small, with sweet suet, put unto it two or three yolks of eggs, being hard-sod, currants and dates small-shred. Season it with a little cinnamon and ginger, a very little cloves and mace, with a little salt and sugar, and a litle thyme finely shred. Make your paste fine with butter and yolks of eggs and sugar, roll it very thin, and so lay it in a platter with butter underneath, and so cut your cover and lay it upon it.

The Good Huswifes Handmaide for the Kitchin (1594)

Chicken Florentine

This is a good recipe for using leftover cold meat.

250 g/9 oz cold cooked chicken
50 g/2 oz suet
Dried fruit to taste
Pinch each of ground cinnamon, ginger, cloves and mace
Salt and pepper
1 egg
1 quantity of shortcrust pastry (page 81)
1 egg to glaze

Mince the chicken and cut the dried fruit into small pieces. Mix all the ingredients and bind with the beaten egg.

Roll out the pastry so as to cover a dinner plate, leaving enough for a pastry top of similar size. Fill the tart base with the meat mixture and cover with the pastry top. This forms a shallow covered tart rather than a deep pie. Brush with beaten egg and bake in the oven at 190°C/375°F/gas mark 5 for 40 minutes or until nicely browned.

Curd tart

A tart is a pie of the third kind: an open pie in which the filling is not covered by a pastry lid. Apple tarts are another of the far-fetched metaphors with which Petruchio startles Kate in *The Taming of the Shrew*. This time it is her sleeve that he has decided he doesn't like:

What's this, a sleeve? 'Tis like a demi-cannon.
What, up and down carved like an apple-tart?

Like fresh milk, curds and whey were not a familiar everyday food in a city such as London. They were the beginning of the process by which milk is turned into a product that keeps well and is of far greater economic value: cheese.

Malmsey, called for in the following recipe, was a heavy, sweet wine from Greece (see page 24). No such wine now comes to England from Greece, but the same grape variety was long ago transplanted to Madeira; hence the Madeira wine that we now call Malmsey will be an excellent substitute.

To make a curde tarte. Take cream, yolks of eggs, white bread, seethe them together, then put in a saucerful of rosewater or Malmsey, and turn it: and put it into a cloth, when all the whey is out, strain it, and put in cinnamon, ginger, salt and sugar, then lay it in paste.

The Good Huswifes Handmaide for the Kitchin (1594)

Curd tart

Various curd tarts are familiar in English regional cookery today – we have seen a Yorkshire curd tart demonstrated to a group of Frenchwomen with much appreciation.

225 g/8 oz curd cheese
2 eggs
125 g/4 oz sugar
50 g/2 oz currants
Small knob of melted butter
Pinch of nutmeg
Zest of 1 lemon
¹/₂ quantity of shortcrust pastry (page 81)

Line an 18-cm/7-inch flan tin with the pastry. Mix all the other ingredients together and pour into the pastry case. Bake in a preheated oven at 180°C/350°F/gas mark 4 for 30 minutes or until set (test by pressing in the middle).

Baked fruits

Apples have been discussed already. Pears are the second typical tree fruit of England, and like apples they were introduced by the Romans. Like apples, too, fresh pears – raw pears – made the dietary writers very nervous. 'If any be so greedy of them that needs they will eat raw pears', Thomas Cogan warns, 'it shall be good to drink after them a draught of old wine of good savour, as sack or Canary wine.' There is nothing wrong with this idea – substitute sweet sherry for Canary – but few would now think it compulsory.

Cogan also names a specific variety, one that had been familiar in England for several centuries before Shakespeare's time. 'Pear-wardens may be longest preserved', he advises, and adds that they are best roasted, baked or stewed; unlike other pears, they were not good to eat fresh. 'I would have had him roasted like a warden in brown paper', says a character in Beaumont and Fletcher's *Cupid's Revenge*, thinking of an uncomfortable form of execution. A warden was a large, late-ripening, long-keeping cooking pear ('warden' may possibly have meant 'keeping', like the French phrase *poire de garde*). If the warden was ever a single variety, it eventually became a generic name for a whole group of orchard pears. Two varieties still sometimes grown, Black Worcester and Parkinson's Warden, are thought to resemble sixteenth-century warden pears.

Quinces, familiar in Mediterranean Europe since ancient times, have been grown in England since 1275 and were well known by the early fifteenth century (when an English cookery book, *Potages dyvers*, gives a recipe for 'Quyncis or wardouns in past', already not unlike the two recipes quoted overleaf). Another useful way with quinces is suggested by Thomas Elyot: 'roasted or sodden [boiled], the core taken out, and mixed with honey clarified or sugar: then they cause good appetite and preserve the head from drunkenness.'

Incidentally, quinces can be used in place of apples in a modern mincemeat recipe. Mincemeat was historically a filling containing minced liver or beef (hence the name) as well as dried fruit and spices. In Shakespeare's time 'shred pies' or 'minced pies' (not very different from chewets, see page 82) were already popular: they were on the way to being a typical Christmas delicacy. Later recipe books sometimes offer one version of mince pies that includes meat and another without any meat for fast days. These two historical types can be seen as forerunners of modern mince pies, sometimes made with beef suet and sometimes with vegetarian suet.

Two pears on a branch (detail). Print from a series after Jacques Le Moyne, published in Paris in 1586. Hand-coloured woodcut, 7.5 x 6.5 cm (image). British Museum, PD 1952,0522.1.47, bequeathed by Sir Hans Sloane.

How to bake wardens. Core your wardens and pare them, and parboil them and lay them in your paste, and put in every warden where you take out the core a clove or twain, put to them sugar, ginger, cinnamon, more cinnamon than ginger, make your crust very fine and somewhat thick, and bake them leisurely. How to bake quinces. Take half a pound of sugar, and a dozen of quinces and pare them, take half an ounce of cinnamon and ginger, take fine flour, sweet butter, and eggs, and make your paste, then put in all your stuff and close it up. Another to bake quinces. Core your quinces and fair pare them, parboil them in seething liquor, wine or water, or half wine and half water, and season them with cinnamon and sugar, and put half a dozen cloves into your pies amongst them, and half a dozen spoonful of rosewater, put in good of sugar. If you will bake them a slighter way, you may put in Muscatel to spare sugar.

A Book of Cookrye (1591)

Winter pears poached in cider

We have inherited two very large pear trees at the bottom of our orchard. A hard hat is needed at harvesting time as each pear may weigh in at 1 lb (½ kg). We have planted a quince alongside the pears. Cooking pears – modern representatives of the warden – and quinces can be dealt with very much alike. Both are inedible when raw and need pre-cooking before adding to a pie etc. Winter pears are perfect for slow poaching in liquor.

4 medium-sized cooking pears
400 ml/14 fl oz/1³/₄ cups cider
4 cloves or piece of cinnamon stick

Peel, core and halve the pears. Put them in a saucepan with all the other ingredients. Cover and poach gently for about 40 minutes until the pears are tender. Remove the spice and serve hot or cold with cream.

Baked quinces or pears

Quinces do well in a slow oven. Peel, core and slice and cover with a little water and a sprinkling of sugar. Bake until soft, at least 45 minutes. Cooking pears are treated likewise, adding either ground ginger or fresh ginger with the water.

Metheglin

Metheglin is one of the relatively few English words that everyone agrees are of Welsh origin. In Welsh *meddyglyn* means literally 'medicinal liquor'; in practice, both in Welsh and in English, it is a name for mead with added spices to give it additional health benefits. The fact that metheglin and mead begin with the same syllable is pure coincidence: mead is an Anglo-Saxon name for a product that was familiar all over northern Europe.

Where grapes ripen well there is no need to make mead, because grape juice is easier to get in quantity than honey or any other conceivable substitute. Where there is no wine, mead, made from honey diluted in water and fermented, is a possible alternative, not quite as easy to make as ale or cider but capable of attaining a higher level of alcohol and therefore easier to store. These conditions applied to England and Wales in the early medieval period, when there was no home-grown wine and not much trade with France. Mead remained moderately popular even later, when more wine was arriving from the south: it tasted good and was known to be healthy. 'Mead, perfectly made, cleanseth the breast and lungs, causeth a man to spit easily and to piss abundantly, and purgeth the belly moderately', writes Thomas Elyot in *The Castel of Helth*. 'Metheglyn', he continues, 'which is most used in Wales, by reason of hot herbs boiled with honey, is hotter than mead, and more comforteth a cold stomach.'

Shakespeare names it twice. On one occasion a Welsh character is speaking, Sir Hugh Evans in *The Merry Wives of Windsor*: he describes Falstaff (who else?) as 'given to fornications, and to taverns and sack and wine and metheglins, and to drinkings and swearings and starings, pribbles and prabbles'. Falstaff, tired and humbled, can only answer: 'I am dejected; I am not able to answer the Welsh flannel; ignorance itself is a plummet o'er me', so we shall never know whether he was a devotee of metheglin or whether that was a flight of Evans's imagination. Evans was right about the sack, though.

There were two ways to make metheglin. The first called for water already flavoured with chosen herbs to be mixed with the honey (see the brief quotation overleaf from Tobias Venner's *Via recta ad vitam longam*, 'The straight way to a long life'). The second, simpler method started with a mixture of honey and water, as normal for mead, and called for a bouquet of herbs to be suspended in the already fermented mead while it matured. That is the basis of the main recipe overleaf, from *The Closet of Sir Kenelm Digby Opened*. We could instead

Bee-keeping. Print from a series after Jan van der Straet, published in Antwerp in or after 1578.
Engraving, 21 x 27.6 cm. British Museum, PD 1957,0413.118.

have chosen Sarah Longe's recipe, of about 1610, the earliest known to us; it is unnecessarily complicated, however, and instead we had recourse to Sir Kenelm, the great expert on mead and metheglin. He died, aged sixty-two, in 1665; his personal recipe book, compiled in the course of a busy life and containing at least twenty variants on metheglin, was published in 1669.

To make white metheglin. Take a gallon of honey; put to it four gallons of water; stir them well together, and boil them in a kettle, till a gallon be wasted with boiling and scumming. Then put it into a vessel to cool. When it is almost as cold as ale-wort, then clear it out into another vessel: then put barm upon it, as you do to your ale, and so let it work. And then turn it up into a vessel, and put into it a bag with ginger, cloves and cinnamon bruised a little, and so hang the bag in the vessel, and stop it up very close; and when it hath stood a month or six weeks, bottle it up and so drink it. You may put in a little lemon-peel into some of your metheglin, for those that like that taste, which most persons do very much.

The Closet of the Eminently Learned Sir Kenelme Digbie Kt. Opened (1669)

[Metheglin.] If rosemary, hyssop, thyme, oregano and sage be first well boiled in the water whereof you make the metheglin, it will be the better.

Tobias Venner, *Via recta ad vitam longam* (1620)

Home-made mead

Nearly all the 'mead' that is sold commercially is not made in the traditional way: it is wine flavoured with honey, and is very sweet. If you prefer to make a metheglin using commercial mead, choose your spices and follow the same method suggested in this book for ipocras (page 43).

Mead that you make yourself is likely to resemble a strong dry white wine, and it is best to make metheglin as a variant of the process of making home-made mead – this is indeed what the seventeenth-century authors advise.

If you make your own mead you will already know about the options: whether to begin by boiling the liquid, or heating without boiling, or not heating at all; whether to add wine yeast or baker's yeast.

If you don't already make it but want to, take 2 kg/4½ lb new liquid honey, 3½ litres/6¼ pints water and blend the two by stirring and bringing to the boil. Skim; continue to skim while you allow the mixture to cool. Before it is quite cold add baker's yeast ('barm' as Sir Kenelm Digby calls it). Leave to ferment in a covered vessel ('let it work' says Sir Kenelm). This fermentation will take three weeks or more, longer than cider and much longer than wine. When the fermentation slows, rack the new mead into a clean vessel which must be filled and must be closed with an airlock. Allow the slow fermentation to finish completely (this will take several more weeks) before bottling. That's mead. Make mead first – it's well worth it – before experimenting with metheglin.

Metheglin

For metheglin, which is spiced mead, you can go with Tobias Venner's method or with Sir Kenelm Digby's (though, to be fair to them, each was well aware of both methods). Venner's method is to boil selected herbs in the water which you will afterwards blend with the honey; Sir Kenelm begins with fresh water. In both cases you will then suspend spices and possibly additional herbs, as you choose, in the new mead at the last production stage, during the slow fermentation. It is the spices that will give the most noticeable flavour elements. Spices often used are root ginger, cinnamon and juniper berries; notice Sir Kenelm's addition of lemon zest. Don't over-spice, and be prepared to remove some or all of the herbs and spices well before the fermentation stops. Your metheglin will be dry, and sugar is a good flavour enhancer, so you may prefer to stir in sugar when drinking. Falstaff would certainly have done the same.

The ghost of
Banquo (detail),
by Théodore
Chassériau. 1854.
Oil on canvas,
54 x 65.3 cm.
Musée des Beaux-
Arts, Reims.

'Fail not our feast'

MACBETH

The banquet scene in *Macbeth* is the most uncomfortable in
any Shakespeare play, a pivot in the development of the plot, an
unforgettable image of the weakness of Macbeth and the steely
determination of his queen.

The former Lord Chamberlain's Servants were now the King's
Servants, taken under his personal patronage by King James I soon
after his arrival in London in 1603. They were, it is thought, keen
to perform a play relevant to James's Scottish background. If so,
Macbeth filled the bill. Its topic was admittedly civil strife and
dynastic murder, as was true of so many historical tragedies, but
in this case, fortunately, the murderous Macbeth, usurper of the
kingdom of Scotland, had been overthrown eventually. It could be
argued that right had prevailed. Banquo, not Macbeth, was James I's
ancestor.

The banquet scene is at the very centre of the intrigue, but
Shakespeare did not put it there. The story was already told in
much the same way in all three of the histories of Scotland that a
seventeenth-century reader might encounter. Hector Boece and
George Buchanan tell it in Latin; Raphael Holinshed spices it up in

English, and Holinshed's *Chronicles* were Shakespeare's favourite source on British history. The witches, the three 'weird sisters' in Holinshed's words, are already part of this historical record. They warn Macbeth that Banquo's offspring, not his own, are fated to inherit the kingdom. Already guilty of murder, he now needs to kill Banquo and his son Fleance. He invites Banquo to supper ('Fail not our feast!') and sends men to assassinate the pair before they arrive.

Hence the empty chair. A banquet prepared, the stage directions in the First Folio tell us. Why a banquet, when Macbeth has invited his lords to supper? Because (in seventeenth-century England, though not in eleventh-century Scotland) a banquet was the dessert that followed supper, and a banquet, with its cakes, sweetmeats and sugar shapes, was static and easy to stage. There would be no need for a boar's head.

Given this setting, the rest is Shakespeare's. It is a beautifully judged scene. No sooner has Macbeth greeted his assembled guests and chosen his own seat –

Lead-glazed earthenware puzzle-tyg, jug and plate. Made in London, 17th century. British Museum, P&E 1925,0401.1.CR (puzzle-tyg), given by Fenton and Sons, P&E 1887,0307,D.24 (jug), P&E 1896,0201.56 (plate), both given by Sir Augustus Wollaston Franks.

'You know your own degrees. Sit down.
At first and last, the hearty welcome . . .
Be large in mirth. Anon we'll drink a measure
The table round.'

– than the killers appear to make their report. He hurries to the
doorway. His first words are: 'There's blood upon thy face!' ''Tis
Banquo's then', the murderer replies, 'his throat is cut', admitting,
a moment later, that young Fleance has escaped. Knowing this,
Macbeth cannot relax, but Lady Macbeth imperiously calls him back
to join the party. In Verdi's opera *Macbeth* she will sing a *brindisi* or
drinking song at this point, *Si colmi il calice di vino eletto*, but there's
really no need: plain words are quite enough. Food can be swallowed
down at home, she tells him; away from home, a proper feast
requires a generous and ceremonious host: 'My Royal Lord, you do
not give the cheer! . . . To feed were best at home: from thence, the
sauce to meat is ceremony.'

And now, as Macbeth turns to sit down, he finds his place taken.
No one else can see the ghostly intruder. Lord Ross nudges him:

'Pleas't your Highness
To grace us with your Royal company?'
'The table's full.' 'Here is a place reserved, Sir.'
'Where?' 'Here, my good Lord. What is't that moves your
Highness?'

Macbeth abandons the argument and addresses Banquo's silent
ghost: 'Thou canst not say I did it! Never shake thy gory locks at
me!' Ross, horrified to see Macbeth apparently talking at random to
an empty seat, reacts: 'Gentlemen, rise. His Highness is not well . . ..'
Lady Macbeth seizes control once more: 'Sit, worthy friends. My Lord
is often thus, and hath been from his youth. Pray you keep seat!' She
snaps at her husband: 'Feed, and regard him not. Are you a man?'
'Ay, and a bold one', Macbeth retorts, but this is the beginning of his
inexorable collapse.

There is no time in this tightly plotted scene to tell us what's on
the table. Strangely enough another play acted by the King's Servants
during these same years fills the gap here. *The Witch*, by Thomas

Middleton, fed on the sudden fashion for theatrical witchcraft that *Macbeth* had started. The setting this time is not medieval Scotland but medieval central Europe, and the scene opens with 'a banquet set out'. Most of the guests are drunk: there have been toasts in 'good Malaga' and there will be more yet. A wedding is being celebrated, and the bridegroom's mistress is too distressed to show her face. The steward tells her it won't be so bad: 'He means to keep you too!' 'How, sir?' 'He doth indeed, he swore 't to me last night.' Then he offers something more substantial in the way of consolation:

'Please you withdraw yourself to yond private parlour:
I'll send you venison, custard, parsnip-pie;
For banqueting stuff, as suckets, jellies, syrups,
I will bring in myself.'

A nice selection from supper is followed by 'banqueting stuff' as dessert. Here we are given the menu for a Shakespearean feast, such as Macbeth's guests might have expected, reduced to manageable size.

Salmon

A salmon was a fine fish, a rare prize: Iago, in his criticism of female inconstancy, hopes that there are some who will refuse to 'change the cod's head for the salmon's tail', that is, to exchange the mere man they have for the nobleman they can't really catch.

England was a good place for fish. Andrew Boorde in his diet handbook, *A Compendyous Regyment*, still popular in Shakespeare's time, writes: 'Of all nations and countries England is best served for fish, not only of all manner of sea-fish but also of freshwater fish, and of all manner and sorts of salt fish.' This was fortunate, because every Friday and the whole of Lent were fast days for those who obeyed the religious rule (as nearly everyone did). Fast days were very largely fish days, and contemporary texts give us long and enticing lists of dishes that were suitable for serving on these days. How to choose? Those

Fish on a seashore, including perch and salmon. Print by Adriaen Collaert, published by Theodoor Galle, after 1598. Engraving, 13 x 18.5 cm. British Museum, PD 1972,U.29.2, bequeathed by Sir Hans Sloane.

who took dietary recommendations seriously could read what Thomas Cogan had to say on the subject: 'I say, of freshwater fish, that to be best which is bred in the deep waters, running swiftly towards the north, stony in the bottom, clean from weeds, whereunto runneth no filth or ordure coming from towns or cities.' Without mentioning the word salmon there could be no clearer recommendation of river-caught salmon than this.

To seeth fresh salmon. Take a little water, and as much beer and salt, and put thereto parsley, thyme and rosemary, and let all these boil together: then put in your salmon, and make your broth sharp with some vinegar.

The Good Huswifes Handmaide for the Kitchin (1594)

Poached salmon

A whole salmon or a fillet from one side
Enough white wine and water to cover
Salt and pepper
Sprigs of parsley, thyme and rosemary

Heat the liquid in a shallow pan, or fish kettle if using a whole fish. Add the fish and simmer gently until just cooked. The liquor can make an accompanying sauce. Since the original sixteenth-century recipe wants a sharp broth I think a sorrel sauce would be a good accompaniment.

Sorrel sauce

Wilt quickly 2 handfuls of tender sorrel leaves in a pan with a smear of olive oil. Chop finely. Heat 250 ml/8¾ fl oz/1 cup crème fraîche until boiling point is reached, then remove the pan from the heat and add the sorrel. Add 4 tablespoons of the fish liquor and serve with the poached salmon. We choose crème fraîche because this ensures the sauce has sharpness.

Spinach tart

Spinach was something of a novelty in Shakespeare's England. William Turner in his *Herbal* (volume 3, 1568) says that 'spinage or spinech is an herb lately found and not long in use'. This doesn't mean that it was discovered growing wild, but that it had only recently been introduced to England from the south. Native to Iran, completely unknown to the Romans, spinach was spread westwards by the Arabs as they conquered North Africa and Spain; slowly it spread northwards from there across France and the rest of Europe.

The writers on diet in Shakespeare's time had just begun to get to grips with it. It is 'cold and moist of complexion', writes Henry Lyte, and 'is sowen in gardens among pot herbs', but he admits uncertainty whether it should be classified as a 'pot herb or rather salad herb'. He adds the observation that spinach 'doth loose the belly', and he is right: it is slightly laxative.

To make a tarte of spinage. Take spinach and parboil it tender, then take it up, and wring out the water clean, and chop it very small, and set it upon the fire with sweet butter in a frying pan, and season it, and set it in a platter to cool, then fill up your tart and so bake it.

A Proper New Booke of Cookery (1575)

Spinach pie

Spinach pie, *fyllo* pastry replacing the shortcrust, is nowadays a Greek speciality (and we have tasted an equally good lettuce pie on Paros in the Cyclades).

1 quantity of shortcrust pastry (page 81)
500 g/1 lb 2 oz spinach
2 tablespoons each of chopped dill, mint and parsley
1 chopped onion
2 chopped cloves of garlic
100 g/3¹/₂ oz feta cheese
Salt and pepper
1 egg to glaze

Remove any tough stalks from the spinach and coarsely chop and add the herbs. Fry off the onion and garlic in olive oil in a large pan. Add the spinach and mix well. Season. Cook in the pan for a further 3 minutes.

Divide the prepared pastry in two, roll out one half and line a large ovenproof dinner plate. Fill with the spinach mixture and dot with crumbled feta cheese. Roll out the second portion to be a cover. Seal the edges well. Brush with a beaten egg. Prick the top. Bake in a preheated oven at 180°C/350°F/gas mark 4 for about 40 minutes.

Mallard with onions

'Goose-flesh and duck-flesh is not praised, except it be a young green goose', Andrew Boorde advises. 'Duck is hotter than goose, and hard to digest, and maketh worse juice', Thomas Elyot confirms, but then adds a rider: 'The brawns on the breastbone and the neck is better than the remnant.' And Thomas Cogan says just the same, adding a not-very-helpful explanation: 'They feed oftentimes of frogs and toads, wherefore their flesh must needs be unwholesome.' Taking no notice of all this, Elizabethan cooks approved of mallard both wild and tame (the same species whose colouring we admire under the name mallard is the one whose meat we usually eat under the name duck). Notice, in the recipe quoted here, the instruction to 'save the dripping'. Duck fat was much too good to waste.

To boyle a mallard with onions. Take a mallard, roast him half enough, and save the dripping, then put him into a fair pot, and his gravy with him, and put into his belly six or seven whole onions, and a spoonful of whole pepper, and as much abroad in your pot, put to it as much mutton broth or beef broth as will cover the mallard, and half a dish of sweet butter, two spoonfuls of verjuice, and let them boil the space of an hour. Then put in some salt, and take off the pot, and lay the mallard upon sops, and the onions about him, and pour the uppermost of the broth upon them.

The Good Huswifes Handmaide for the Kitchin (1594)

To make sops for chickens. First take butter, and melt it upon a chafing-dish with coals, and lay in the dish thin toasts of bread, and make sorrel sauce with verjuice and gooseberries, seethe them with a little verjuice and lay them upon.

The Good Huswifes Handmaide for the Kitchin (1594)

The duck hunt (detail). Print in the style of Virgil Solis. German, c. 1530–40. Woodcut, 12 x 40 cm. British Museum, PD 1942,0820.1.

Duck with onions

1 duck (about 2 kg/4½ lb) or 4 duck joints
4 medium onions
50 g/2 oz butter
2 rashers bacon
Rind of 1 orange
1 bouquet garni
Salt and pepper
2 tablespoons verjuice
500 ml/1 pint/2 cups chicken stock
150 ml/5 fl oz/²⁄₃ cup red wine
40 g/1½ oz plain flour

Joint the duck and trim away any excess fat. Dust in seasoned flour and brown, using half the butter, in a large pan. Remove to a casserole. Melt the remaining butter in the frying pan and brown the chopped bacon with the roughly chopped onions. Remove to the casserole and add the bouquet garni and the grated orange rind. Deglaze the pan with stock and verjuice and add to the casserole. Cover with a well-fitting lid and cook for about 1 hour, then add the red wine and continue cooking, uncovered, for an extra 30 minutes in an oven at 180°C/350°F/gas mark 4.

Red marmalade

Quinces were used extensively, as were pears and apples, for baking in pies, jellies and marmalades, and also in sauces for meat dishes. They are less well known these days, no doubt because they demand more preparation, but they impart a special flavour and perfume.

'Marmalade' now means a citrus fruit preserve, usually orange. It once meant specifically and exclusively a quince preserve. This was a Portuguese speciality (in Portuguese *marmelo* means 'quince') which became popular in England in the early sixteenth century. At first marmalade was imported from Portugal or Spain. Then, as quinces spread in English orchards, *marmelett* began to be made at home. There are many recipes in early cookbooks, but essentially only one method, because this is simply the best way to develop the full flavour and rich colour of this unique fruit. It is important to use the cores because the pips contain pectin.

Thomas Cogan, in *The Haven of Health*, recommends adding rose water, or a proportion of apples, both of which change the flavour and aroma. Try these ideas if you like, but we agree with Mrs Longe: a pure quince marmalade is unbeatable.

Red marmelett. Take quinces and pare them, quarter them and core them. Then take a pound of them and a pound of sugar and half a pint of water, and put all in a skillet; and when it is hot take a good many of the cores of the quinces and tie them up in a piece of lawn and put them in. Then cover them and let them boil softly for 2 hours. Then take out the cores and wring them between two trenchers; and then break the quinces, and cover them, and let them boil apace, and stir them till they be enough. And so put it into boxes.

Mrs. Sarah Longe her Receipt Booke (c. 1610)

Quinces and a caterpillar. Drawing from an album by Jacques Le Moyne. *c.* 1585. Watercolour and bodycolour, 21.5 x 13.8 cm. British Museum, PD 1962,0714.1.38, purchased with assistance from the Pilgrim Trust and the Art Fund.

Quince marmalade

We keep this marmalade in the fridge until needed, whether as a spread, in tarts or as a sweet to serve with cheese. It is firm enough to cut into squares or slices. Quince marmalade made by this method is still popular in France, Spain and Portugal.

1 kg/2 lb 3 oz sugar for each 1 kg/2 lb 3 oz of quince pulp

Wash, peel and core the quinces. Tie the cores in a muslin cloth and cut the flesh into slices. Cook the quince flesh, plus the muslin bag of cores, until the fruit is soft. This can take 45 minutes to 1 hour. Discard the bag and press the flesh through a sieve. Add sugar corresponding to the weight of the pulp.

Cook gently for about an hour or more, stirring so that the mixture does not stick or burn on the bottom of the saucepan. The pulp will thicken and change to a rich red colour. Pour the pulp into foil containers (freezer containers are ideal) to a depth of 2 to 3 cm. Cover the surface with greaseproof paper and seal the containers.

Gooseberry fool

Gooseberries now seem a very English fruit – they are not much appreciated in France, for example – but, just like quinces, they are not known to have been grown in England before 1275. One of the gooseberry's earliest appearances in literature is on the lips of Sir John Falstaff in *Henry IV part 2*: 'All the other gifts appertinent to man, as the malice of this age shapes them, are not worth a gooseberry.' This doesn't say much in favour of gooseberries – yet they had spread widely by this time: 'The gooseberry is planted commonly almost in every garden of this country alongest the hedges and borders', writes Henry Lyte, adding that the fruit 'is much used in meats . . . it cooleth the vehement heat of the stomach and liver'. They were just beginning to appear in cookery books.

A classic recipe, gooseberry fool, dates from 1610 at the latest, as seen from the quotation below. No one knows why the word 'fool' is used with this meaning. It appears to be a purely English recipe and a purely English name – hinted at by the Fool in *King Lear*, who jokes about how ladies and gentlemen at a banquet will not let him alone but will be 'snatching' at him.

To make a goosebery foole. Take 2 handfuls of green gooseberries, and prick them, then scald them very soft, and pour the water from them very clean, and break them very small, and season them with rosewater and sugar, and then take a quart of cream or butter, and put in a little mace, and set it on the fire (letting it boil) and then take it off, and take out the mace, and pour it into the gooseberries, and stir it about, and let it stand till it be cold, and then eat it.

Mrs. Sarah Longe her Receipt Booke (c. 1610)

Gooseberry fool

Gooseberries are the classic, but other fruits can be used in this way, including medlars (sweetened medlar purée being blended with whipped cream).

300 g/10 oz gooseberries
120 g/4 oz sugar
1/2 teaspoon ground mace
180 ml/6 fl oz/3/4 cup double cream

Bring the berries to the boil with the sugar and mace until they are soft. Push through a sieve (hence there is no need to top and tail the gooseberries in advance). Whip the cream until stiff and fold into the gooseberry purée. Chill in the fridge before serving.

White-pot

White-pot is historically linked with Devon, where in Shakespeare's time some villages used to choose a White-pot Queen on May Day every year. White-pot is still made in the West Country at Whitsuntide; in other parts of England and at other periods a very similar dish has been called frumety or furmity.

Mrs Longe's recipe for white-pot uses sliced bread, and there is a comparable recipe in the *Commonplace Book* of Lady Catherine Grey, but this was not the usual way. Wheat flour is often the cereal basis, as in the modern Gloucestershire recipe that we give below, while Henry Lyte's *A New Herbal* in 1578 notes that 'the meal of buckwheat is used', and the eighteenth-century food writer Hannah Glasse gives a recipe for a rice white-pot.

To make a white-pot. Take a quart of cream, a loaf of bread, and slice it thin (the crust being taken from it), one nutmeg, and stir it, a pound of currants, and set it on the fire a quarter of an hour, and boil it thick (keeping it stirred), and take 7 eggs, and beat them, and take 3 whites from them, and take a quarter of a pound of sugar, put the eggs and sugar into the rest, and boil it, then put it in a dish, and bake it in the oven for the space of an hour; you may put the marrow of 2 bones into it when you put it into the oven, and for want of that you may put in a little slice of butter.

Mrs. Sarah Longe her Receipt Booke (c. 1610)

White-pot

1 litre/1³/₄ pints/4 cups milk
1 tablespoon brown sugar
2 tablespoons treacle or golden syrup
1 tablespoon plain flour
150 ml/5 fl oz/²/₃ cup cold water

Use a deep ovenproof bowl. Beat the flour, treacle and sugar together with a tablespoon or two of the milk. Boil the remainder of the milk and pour into the bowl. At the last moment pour the cold water into the middle of the bowl and put into the oven without stirring. Bake in a gentle oven, 155°C/310°F/gas mark 2–3, for 2 hours.

A milkmaid. Drawing from an album by Adriaen van de Venne. 1620–26. Watercolour and bodycolour over black chalk, 9.6 x 15.1 cm. British Museum, PD 1978,0624.42.53.

June: peasants
shearing sheep
(detail). Print from
a series of the
Twelve Months
by an anonymous
French artist,
c. 1580. Woodcut,
18.1 x 28.3 cm.
British Museum,
PD E,9.168.

'Our sheep-shearing feast'

THE WINTER'S TALE

The Winter's Tale, one of those later Shakespeare comedies that are now categorized as 'problem plays', had its first known performance in 1611. It is set partly in Sicily, partly in Bohemia, which, if names mean anything, should represent the modern Czech Republic, a region that Shakespeare famously equips with a sea coast.

Nearly the whole story, including this geographical setting, is borrowed from *Pandosto*, a story published in 1588 by Robert Greene. Greene (who was also a playwright) is most famous for his attack on the young ill-educated plagiarist Shakespeare, 'an upstart crow, beautified with our feathers'. If this rankled with Shakespeare – and there are signs that he didn't forget it – it didn't stop him borrowing dramatic material out of Greene's writings.

In Greene's story the festivity takes place in Sicily:

It happened not long after this that there was a meeting of all the farmers' daughters in Sicilia, whither Fawnia was also bidden as the

mistress of the feast, who, having attired herself in her best garments, went among the rest of her companions to the merry meeting, there spending the day in such homely pastimes as shepherds use.

The event brings the main characters together at the crucial moment, but nothing more is made of it. Shakespeare takes up the idea that the heroine (now renamed Perdita) will be mistress of the feast, and builds several scenes around the occasion. Her foster-brother is sent to town to buy supplies:

'Let me see, what am I to buy for our sheep-shearing feast? Three pound of sugar, five pound of currants, rice – what will this sister of mine do with rice? But my father hath made her mistress of the feast, and she lays it on. She hath made me four and twenty nosegays for the shearers . . . I must have saffron to colour the warden pies; mace; dates, none, that's out of my note; nutmegs, seven; a race or two of ginger, but that I may beg; four pound of prunes, and as many of raisins o'th' sun.'

Perdita herself, the queen of curds and cream according to one admirer, greets her guests with herbs appropriate to the seasons and to their ages (though the violets, primroses and oxlips of spring are past): 'For you there's rosemary and rue; these keep seeming and savour all the winter long.' Then again:

'Here's flowers for you:
Hot lavender, mints, savory, marjoram;
The marigold that goes to bed with the sun,
And with him rises weeping; these are flowers
Of middle summer, and I think they are given
To men of middle age.'

It makes no difference whether the sheep-shearing feast is set in Sicily as Greene has it, or in Bohemia with Shakespeare. A sheep-shearing feast was not at all exotic. In fact it was a very English thing, still celebrated in sheep-farming districts every June even in the early twentieth century.

Shakespeare happens to focus on the spices that were bought for the occasion: the only specific dish that gets into the dialogue is a warden pie. No more was needed: the audience could fill in the gaps for themselves. Luckily, so can we, because not many years afterwards Ben Jonson, in his last, unfinished play *The Sad Shepherd*, told a story of Robin Hood and set it on the occasion of a sheep-shearing feast. Maid Marion instructs her companions how to enjoy themselves:

Fall to your cheesecakes, curds, and clotted cream,
Your fools, your flans; and of ale a stream
To wash it from your livers! Strain ewes' milk
Into your cider syllabubs, and be drunk
To him whose fleece hath brought the earliest lamb
This year and wears the baldric at your board!

We include elsewhere in this book some of the recipes that Maid Marion has in mind: a curd tart on page 85, a gooseberry fool on page 106, and a cider syllabub on page 134.

Agate bowl. Made in Milan or Prague, early 17th century. H. 7.5 cm. British Museum, P&E WB.84, bequeathed by Baron Ferdinand Anselm de Rothschild.

Roast leg of mutton

Sir Andrew Aguecheek in *Twelfth Night* is proud of his social accomplishments. He dances: 'Faith, I can cut a caper.' 'And I can cut the mutton to't', Toby retorts, food always in mind. Now on this point Lancelot de Casteau, cited on page 116 for his disagreement with an English recipe book, disagrees with Sir Toby Belch. Casteau includes capers (*cappes de Genua*) in his veal hotchpot. Englishmen, like Sir Toby, knew that capers went with mutton.

Hardly known in England before the sixteenth century, capers were becoming familiar through mentions in herbals. 'It groweth not in this country', writes Henry Lyte, 'but the fruit and flowers are knowen unto us, because they be brought to us from Spain preserved in brine or salt.' There was some reluctance among the dietary writers to accept that anything so powerfully flavoured could be safe to eat. Lyte suggests avoiding the pickled fruits, which have the strongest taste, adding that 'the flowers and young leaves . . . serve better to be eaten with meats'. All three can still be found in delicatessens: the fruits or the flower-buds, but not the leaves, would serve for the following recipe. Claret, called for here, was any light-coloured red wine (not necessarily Bordeaux).

To roast a legge of mutton on the French fashion. Pare all the skin as thin as you can: lard it with sweet lard, and stick about it a dozen cloves: when it is half roasted, cut off three or four thin pieces, and mince it small, with a few sweet herbs, and a little beaten ginger. Put in a ladleful of claret wine, a piece of sweet butter, two or three spoonfuls of verjuice, a little pepper, a few parboiled capers: when all this is boiled together, chop the yolk of an hard egg into it. Then dredge your leg, and serve it upon sauce.

John Murrell, *A New Booke of Cookerie* (1615)

Roast leg of lamb

Hugh Fearnley-Whittingstall rightly observes that 'mutton is to lamb what beef is to veal'. Mutton is not so much appreciated just now, so the modern version of this recipe is for roast leg of lamb.

1 leg of lamb
3 cloves of garlic cut into slivers
Olive oil
Handful of parsley
100 ml/3^1/$_2$ fl oz/^{1}/$_2$ cup red wine
2 tablespoons verjuice (or more to taste)
Salt and pepper
Handful of caper buds

Lard the lamb with slivers of garlic to taste, rub with olive oil and roast according to weight: set the joint in a hot oven at 220°C/425°F/gas mark 7 for half an hour and then reduce heat to 180°C/350°F/gas mark 4 and give it 35 minutes for each 500 g/1 lb 2 oz of weight, or until the juices run clear when pierced with a skewer. Halfway through the cooking mix parsley, wine, verjuice, seasoning and capers and pour over the lamb to finish cooking.

At the end of cooking remove the lamb to rest and make a gravy with the pan juices and flour in the traditional way.

French potage

'Potage is not so much used in all Christendom as it is used in England', writes Andrew Boorde. This is strange, because potage was a French word, one of the many that crossed the Channel with William the Conqueror's Norman warriors and spread into the Anglo-Saxon vernacular, where it became the proper term for a whole class or category of culinary expertise. When a gentleman considers employing a cook, Thomas Elyot advises, he must 'examine him, how many sorts of meats, potages and sauces he can perfectly make'.

Andrew Boorde goes on to define the English potage as he knows it: it is made 'of the liquor in the which flesh is sodden in' – boiled in, that is – with chopped herbs, oatmeal and salt. The herbs, 'if they be pure, good and clean . . . doth comfort many men'. In earlier centuries, likewise, potage was known to be a health-giving food for invalids, much used in monasteries. Whether Boorde is really correct in his claim that potage was commonest in England is hard to say. Lancelot de Casteau's contemporary *Ouverture de cuisine* is full of dishes *en potage*, all the way from *cerf* (venison) to *choux fleuris* (cauliflowers). The only variation that seems to be missing, oddly enough, is the very one that is called a 'French pottage' in the following recipe: Casteau offers no version of lamb or mutton *en potage*.

How to make a French pottage. Take the ribs of mutton, chop them small, the bones and all with the flesh, in square pieces. Then take carrot roots, and for lack of them, onions, or both together an if you will, or else herbs such as you like: seethe all these together, and when you will serve it in, season your pot with a little cinnamon, pepper and salt, and so serve it forth.

The Good Huswifes Handmaide for the Kitchin (1594)

Farmers with their produce. Print after Pieter Aertsen, from a series by Jacob Matham published in Haarlem in 1603. Engraving, 23.8 x 33.5 cm. British Museum, PD 1856,0209.292.

Spring vegetable soup (Potage aux primeurs)

This modern French potage is made from the first vegetables of the season. One could substitute other vegetables to taste or as available, including for example celery and young turnip. If using not fresh but frozen peas in this recipe, add them 5 minutes before the end of the cooking time.

3 leeks cut in strips
1 medium lettuce cut in strips
4 tablespoons chopped fresh herbs such as parsley, sorrel and purslane
150 g/5 oz green peas or tender broad beans
1¹/₂ litres/2¹/₂ pints stock
Salt and pepper
¹/₂ teaspoon ground cinnamon
4 egg yolks

Wash and drain the leek and lettuce strips. Heat the stock and add the leek, lettuce, chopped herbs and peas. Season with salt, pepper and the cinnamon. Simmer for 15 minutes or until the vegetables are tender. Whisk the 4 egg yolks in a small bowl and blend in 3 spoonfuls of the soup. Take the soup off the heat and whisk in the egg mixture, stirring all the time. Check the seasoning and serve.

Friday pie

The *Oxford English Dictionary* hasn't heard of Friday pies, though it knows of Friday fare and a Friday feast. The Friday pie of John Murrell's recipe will be suitable for vegetarians and for the strictest fast, excluding as it does both meat and fish.

'Well relished' apples, in the following recipe, are those with a good strong flavour; a 'coffin' is a pie case (see page 80). 'Raisins of the sun', also mentioned in the list of spices to be bought at market for the sheep-shearing feast in *The Winter's Tale*, were the largest grade of raisins, so called because they were sun-dried. 'Raisins do make the stomach firm and strong', writes Thomas Elyot, 'and do provoke appetite, and do comfort weak bodies, being eaten afore meals.'

A Fridayes pye, without eyther flesh or fish. Wash green beets clean, pick out the middle string, and chop them small with two or three well relished ripe apples. Season it with pepper, salt and ginger: then take a good handful of raisins of the sun, and put all in a coffin of fine paste, with a piece of sweet butter, and so bake it: but before you serve it in, cut it up, and wring in the juice of an orange, and sugar.

John Murrell, A New Booke of Cookerie (1615)

Friday pie

Prepare a shortcrust pastry case as for spinach pie (see page 101), and use the same method, replacing the ingredients as follows. In place of spinach one can use chard (beet) leaves or kale. De-vein them and chop up finely. Chopped dessert apple, a pinch of mace and salt and pepper can be added with knobs of butter. I like to use orange juice, squeezed over the green leaves before the pie is sealed.

Short pastry for a tart

Pastry is 'short' (this technical term has been used in English cookery books since the early fifteenth century) if it crumbles quickly – if it makes a short mouthful, in fact. Which must be why it doesn't take long to eat a shortcake.

To make short paste for a Tart. Take fine flour, a little fair water, and a dish of sweet butter, and a little saffron, and the yolks of two eggs, and make it thin and as tender as ye may.

A Proper New Booke of Cookery (1575)

Short pastry for a tart

Use the shortcrust pastry recipe on page 81, add a good pinch of saffron to the flour before rubbing in the butter. This is the pastry to be used for a warden pie (see original recipes on page 89).

Cambridge pudding

A pudding was historically an animal's stomach stuffed with minced meat or suet and other ingredients, then boiled or baked: a haggis is therefore a pudding, and the word is still used in this sense in the modern black pudding. Or, sometimes, it was the 'stuffing', the ingredients with which a whole animal was stuffed before roasting: hence the comparison of Falstaff to a 'roasted Manningtree ox with the pudding in his belly'.

Dish of fruit. Drawing from an album by Jacques Le Moyne. c. 1585. Watercolour and bodycolour, 14.3 x 16.4 cm. British Museum, PD 1962,0714.1.51, purchased with assistance from the Pilgrim Trust and the Art Fund.

We include this recipe, we admit, partly because we once lived in Cambridge. But as to why the recipe is called a Cambridge pudding we cannot make any suggestion. Cambridge, then as now, was best known as a University town, and its college kitchens no doubt had their specialities then as now: possibly this was one. To searce, in this recipe, is to sift or sieve.

A Cambridge pudding. Searce grated bread through a colander, mince it with flour, minced dates, currants, nutmeg, cinnamon, and pepper, minced suet, new milk warm, fine sugar, and eggs: take away some of their whites, work all together. Take half the pudding on the one side, and the other on the other side, and make it round like a loaf. Then take butter, and put it in the midst of the pudding, and the other half aloft. Let your liquor boil, and throw your pudding in, being tied in a fair cloth: when it is boiled enough cut it in the midst, and so serve it in.

John Murrell, *A New Booke of Cookerie* (1615)

Cambridge pudding

This is basically a steamed suet pudding with dried fruit; there is also a resemblance to pond pudding with the well of butter inside.

110 g/4 oz breadcrumbs
50 g/2 oz self-raising flour
50 g/2 oz muscovado (dark brown) sugar
75 g/3 oz suet
Salt
140 g/5 oz mixed dried fruits of your choice
1 teaspoon each ground cinnamon and nutmeg
2 eggs; a little milk if needed
30 g/1 oz butter, cut into knobs

Butter a 1-litre pudding basin. Combine the breadcrumbs, flour, pinch of salt, sugar, fruits, spices and suet in a large bowl. Beat the 2 eggs and stir into the mixture. Blend well; if it is too dry add a little milk. Tip half the mixture into the pudding basin and add the knobs of butter before tipping in the remaining mixture. Cover with a pleated piece of greaseproof paper and a layer of foil. Steam for at least 2 hours.

King Henry VIII, act I scene 4 (detail). Print from a series made by Isaac Taylor, published in London in 1798. Etching and engraving, 50.4 x 63.5 cm. British Museum, PD Dd,6.27.

'An idle banquet'

KING HENRY VIII

Not everyone manages to see a performance of Shakespeare's *King Henry VIII*: it isn't among the perennial favourites. Those who are lucky should look out for the masked ball and banquet at Cardinal Wolsey's (act I scene 4). In all of Shakespeare's work there are few more romantic moments.

To begin with, this supper and dance seems to be a real event. It is described, dated to 30 December 1526, in the expanded edition of Raphael Holinshed's *Chronicles*:

That same night, the King and many young gentlemen with him, came to Bridewell, and there put him and fifteen other, all in masquing apparel, and then took his barge, and rowed to the Cardinal's place, where were at supper a great company of lords and ladies. And then the masquers danced and made goodly pastime; and when they had well danced, the ladies plucked away their visors, and so they were all known, and to the King was made a great banquet.

Shakespeare was a keen reader of Holinshed, his main source for the Macbeth story as well as several history plays. Here he found just

what he needed for the climax of act I – an occasion for Henry to meet Anne Boleyn. What better moment than this post-Christmas celebration, suddenly interrupted by masked revellers, one of whom turns out to be the king himself?

In the play, the strangers are reported to Wolsey as a party of 'great ambassadors from foreign princes who speak no English'. With an apologetic word to his invited guests ('You have now a broken banquet, but we'll mend it. A good digestion to you all!'), he calls the newcomers in. They join the revelry, and the disguised Henry dances with Anne. Then they are all unmasked, and Henry finds the opportunity to ask:

'My Lord Chamberlain,
Prithee come hither. What fair lady's that?'
'An't please your Grace, Sir Thomas Boleyn's daughter
The Viscount Rochford, one of her Highness' women.'
'By Heaven, she is a dainty one. Sweet heart,
I were unmannerly to take you out
And not to kiss you. A health, gentlemen!
Let it go round!'

Toasts had been the occasion for some suggestive banter even before the masquers' arrival. Now the wassail-bowl goes round again and a toast serves as pretext for Henry and Anne's first kiss, after which he leads her to the banqueting chamber. Wolsey asks:

'Sir Thomas Lovell, is the banquet ready
I' th' privy chamber?' 'Yes, my lord.' [Wolsey turns to the King:]
'Your Grace,
I fear, with dancing is a little heated?'
'I fear, too much!' 'There's fresher air, my lord,
In the next chamber.' [The King recognizes his cue:]
'Lead in your ladies, every one. Sweet partner,
'I must not yet forsake you. Let's be merry!'

This cleverly contrived incident is prelude to the rest of the plot – the rejection of Catherine of Aragon, the fall of Wolsey and the doomed marriage with Anne herself.

In action the banquet scene was more exciting than the playwright expected. The problem arose at one of the early performances at the Globe Theatre. Working from the published text (1623) we might say that it arose precisely at line 49, where Lord Sandys's last off-colour joke is interrupted by a stage direction: 'Drum and trumpet, chambers discharged.' These 'chambers' (firearms) herald the arrival of the anonymous masquers.

At the performance on 29 June 1613 the old Globe's thatched roof caught fire. Quite clearly it happened at this very moment as a result of the offstage business with gunpowder. As we can see in Henry Wotton's report of the event, the play as yet had a different title, yet it is essentially the same:

The King's Players had a new play, called All Is True, representing some principal pieces of the reign of Henry VIII. King Henry making a masque at the Cardinal Wolsey's house, and certain chambers being shot off at his entry, some of the paper, or other stuff, wherewith one of them was stopped, did light on the thatch, where . . . it kindled inwardly, and ran round like a train, consuming within less than an hour the whole house to the very grounds. Nothing did perish but wood and straw, and a few forsaken cloaks; only one man had his breeches set on fire, that would perhaps have broiled him, if he had not by the benefit of a provident wit put it out with bottle ale.

Gold and jewelled standing cup and cover. Probably made in Transylvania, 17th century. H. 18.5 cm (with cover). British Museum, P&E WB.66, bequeathed by Baron Ferdinand Anselm de Rothschild.

Pike

Pike 'is called the king and tyrant of other fishes, because he not only devoureth fishes of other kinds, but also of his own kind', says Thomas Cogan. 'If the young dace be a bait for the old pike', says Sir John Falstaff, planning to take advantage of Shallow, 'I see no reason in the law of nature but I may snap at him.' Falstaff intends to be the pike in this metaphor.

It is a freshwater fish and a very big one – up to one and a half metres in length and 35 kg in weight – though the biggest are said to be not as good as the middle-sized ones gastronomically. In the following recipe 'sodden' means seethed, i.e. boiled. Sweet butter is fresh and unsalted.

Bay salt is salt from the Bay of Biscay. In the sixteenth century, as today, gourmets evidently liked the savoury, high-priced salts from the Atlantic coast of France, now known as *sel gris* and (the finest quality) *fleur de sel*. This salt may sometimes have a pink tinge from the alga *Dunaliella salina*, which is high in *beta*-carotene. 'Bay salt', although it no longer has this name, comes nowadays from Guérande, Noirmoutier and the Ile de Ré.

To seethe a pike. Scour your pike with bay salt, and then open him on the back, faire wash him, and then cast a little white salt upon him. Set on fair water well seasoned with salt. When this liquor seetheth, then put in your pike and fair scum it, then take the best of the broth when it is sodden, and put it in a little chafer or pipkin, and put thereto parsley and a little thyme, rosemary, whole mace, good yeast, and half as much verjuice as you have liquor, and boil them together, and put in the liver of the pike, and the caul, being clean scaled and washed, and let them boil well, then season your broth with pepper gross beaten, with salt not too much, because your liquor is salt that your pike is boiled in, put therein a good piece of sweet butter, and season it with a little sugar that it be neither too sharpen nor too sweet. So take up your pike and lay it upon sops, the skinny side upward, and so lay your broth upon it.

A Book of Cookrye (1591)

Sauce for pike

'Brook fish' in the following recipe are freshwater fish, and bream (to be distinguished from sea bream) is one of these. Flounder, because they are caught close to the shore and in estuaries, count among freshwater fish in this list. Eels, salmon, and a few sea fish for which the same sauce can be adapted, are mentioned later in the text.

Sauce was commonly thought of as a separate item from the dish with which it was served, not only in the cook's mind but also (at an inn) on the diner's bill. Hence Falstaff's tavern bill, quoted on page 47, lists 'capon' and 'sauce' separately.

A pike sauce: for a pike, bream, perch, roch, carp, flounders, and all manner of brooke fish. Take a posy of rosemary and thyme, and bind them together, and put in also a quantity of parsley not bound, and put it into a cauldron of water, salt, and yeast, and the herbs, and let them boil a pretty while, then put in the fish, and a good quantity of butter, and let them boil a good while, and you shall have your pike sauce. For all these fishes above written if they must be broiled: take sauce for them, butter, pepper and vinegar, and boil it upon a chafing-dish, and then lay the broiled fish upon the dish, but for eels and fresh salmon nothing but pepper and vinegar over-boiled, and also if you will fry them, you must take a good quantity of parsley, after the fish is fried, put in the parsley into the frying pan, and let it fry in the butter, then take it up and put it on the fried fish, as fried plaice, whiting, and such other fish, except eels, fresh salmon and conger, which be never fried, but baked, broiled, roasted and sodden.

A Book of Cookrye (1591)

Sauce for pike and other fish

Make a basic white sauce with the liquor from poaching the fish, add plenty of chopped parsley, seasoning and extra butter to make the sauce glisten. For some kinds of fish you may now want to add vinegar. Pour over the fish.

Sauce for roast rabbit

The following recipe gives us a glimpse of the *nouvelle cuisine* that was practised at King Henry VIII's dinner table: it is a good sauce whose value is partly in the flavours, partly the careful preparation, and, last but not least, the presentation.

As explained on page 50, the words cony and rabbit were partial synonyms, but rabbit was more often used for young animals. In the following recipe it is not clear what is meant; either the serving-dish was very large or the king was being served with roasted baby rabbits.

Fine sauce for a roasted rabbet: used to king Henrie the eight. Take a handful of washed parsley, minced small, boil it with butter and verjuice upon a chafing-dish, season it with sugar, and a litle pepper gross beaten: when it is ready, put in a few crumbs of white bread amongst the others; let it boil again till it be thick: then lay it in a platter, like the breadth of three fingers, lay of each side one roasted cony or more, and so serve them.

The Good Huswifes Handmaide for the Kitchin (1594)

Sauce for roast rabbit

1 tablespoon flour
30 g/1 oz butter
1 tablespoon verjuice
300 ml/10 fl oz/1¹⁄₃ cups stock
Handful of chopped parsley
Pepper

Make a roux with the butter and flour, gradually add the verjuice and stock, stir until thick, then add the parsley and plenty of pepper to taste. Serve alongside roasted rabbit.

Spit-roasted boar

'Neither is all swine's flesh so commendable', writes Thomas Cogan, getting down to details on the subject of pork, 'but that which is young, and best of a year or two old. Also better of a wild swine than of a tame.' This, however, he goes on to admit, is a counsel of perfection, because 'our use in England is for the more part to breed our swine at home'. In these few words he tells us just what we need to know: first, that young wild boars (male or female) are best of all to eat, and few would disagree. Second, that wild boar had become rare (perhaps already extinct) in England, although in earlier centuries there had been more than enough to go round. Third, that what is called wild boar is often not as wild as all that. The real difference Cogan is getting at is not between domesticated and wild but between bred at home and bred in hunting parks. Even in England there were 'wild boars' in this special sense, available, for example, for a king and his noblemen to hunt whenever it took their fancy.

It was a dangerous game. Boars can inflict a potentially deadly injury or cause death indirectly: it was well known that Philip IV of France had died during a boar hunt, though whether the precise cause was a stroke, or an accidental fall from his horse, was disputed.

The proper way to deal with the boar once killed was to cook the head separately, a lengthy and complex operation, to spit-roast the body, and to present both head and body in the dining hall with plaudits to the brave huntsman who had made the kill. We point to the illustration but have no sixteenth-century recipe to quote and don't offer a recipe for these specialized procedures.

Parcel-gilt drinking-cup in the form of a boar. Made by Johannes Lencker in Augsburg, 1601–25. H. 26 cm. British Museum, P&E WB.135, bequeathed by Baron Ferdinand Anselm de Rothschild.

Chaldron of swan

A chaldron or chawder is a sauce or soup that is made from the chopped entrails of an animal; historically it is the same word as chowder. The witches' brew in *Macbeth* (for which we give no full recipe here) includes tiger chawdron among various even more unpleasant ingredients:

Add thereto a tiger's chawdron,
For the ingredience of our cauldron . . .
Cool it with a baboon's blood,
Then the charm is firm and good.

Chaldron was a typical sauce to serve with swan on the relatively few occasions when swan was eaten. The meat itself would be spit-roasted, and the cooked bird would probably be presented whole in the dining-hall, perhaps partly gilded, an elaborate and spectacular procedure. Swan was always expensive, and in Britain at least it is now ruled out as a food except at two tables: that of the Queen (who is the legal owner of all mute swans on English waters) and that of St John's College, Cambridge, which, once a year, maintains its ancient right to kill a swan for a feast. That's where we once ate swan. We prefer turkey, and for this and other reasons we don't offer a modern recipe for chaldron of swan.

Those who prefer not to eat swan are in agreement with Henry Lyte, sixteenth-century translator of the *New Herbal* quoted on page 36. Lyte, lord of the manor of Lyte's Cary in Somerset, believed that when his ancestor, the ancient Trojan Leitus, fled to Britain he brought with him three of the Carian swans of the river Maeander. 'These sacred birds', he wrote, gave a name to Lyte's Cary and were commemorated as the three silver swans on his family coat of arms.

The method suggested in *A Book of Cookrye* is not unlike the making of boudin noir; *boudin de canard* is therefore a close relative of chaldron of swan, and well worth making or tasting.

A game- and fruit-seller's stall. Drawing by Frans Snyders, 1594–1657. Pen and grey ink with watercolour, 27.4 x 42.4 cm. British Museum, PD 1836,0811.511.

Chauldron for a swan. Take white bread and lay it in soak in some of the broth that the giblets be sod in, and strain it with some of the blood of the swan, a little piece of the liver and red wine, and make it somewhat thin, and put to it cinnamon and ginger, pepper, salt and sugar, and boil it until it be somewhat thick, and put in two spoonful of the gravy of the swan, and so serve it in saucers being warm.

A Book of Cookrye (1591)

Maunger blaunche

Blancmanger or *manger blanc*, an admired dish of high status from the fourteenth century to Shakespeare's time and beyond, is – obviously – an ancestor of modern British blancmange. It was a delicately flavoured, rather sweet dish that set like jelly and was eaten, cold, at banquets. There are two big differences, though. First, our modern blancmange is nearly always coloured: sixteenth-century blancmange was white, and quite right too, because the name means 'white food' in French. Secondly, there is no meat (perish the thought) in our modern blancmange, but the basic ingredient of sixteenth-century blancmange was minced capon or chicken breast. Other meat or fish could be substituted, but to maintain the correct colour it must necessarily be white.

As may be seen from the second recipe quoted here, the idea of a blancmange without meat probably originated in the religious rule of a weekly fast. 'Fish day' in the title means 'fast day': it says nothing about the ingredients of the blancmange, which contains no fish. The two forms of blancmange must have continued side by side until the eighteenth century, when blancmange with meat went out of fashion.

In the first of the following recipes morning milk is specified. Milk from the morning milking contained proportionately less cream than evening milk; assuming that one is following this recipe during the day, morning milk was also fresher. Pap, mentioned when the texture is explained, is porridge or bread-and-milk.

To make maunger blaunche. Take half a pound of rice very clean picked and washed, then beat it very fine, and searce it through a fine searce, and put the finest of it in a quart of mornings milk, and strain it through a strainer, and put it in a fair pot, and set it on the fire, but it must be but a soft fire, and still stir it with a broad stick. And when it is a little thick take it from the fire, and take the brawn of a very tender capon, and pull it in as small pieces as ye can, and the capon must be sodden in fair water, and the brawn of it must be pulled as small as a horse-hair with your fingers, and put it into the milk which is but half thickened, and then put in as much sugar as ye think will make it sweet, and put in a dozen spoonfuls of good rosewater, and set it on the fire again, and stir it well, and in the stirring, all to beat it with your stick, from the one side of the pan to the other, and when it is as thick as pap, take it from the fire, and put it in a fair platter, and when it is cold, lay three slices in a dish, and cast a little sugar on it, and so serve it in.

The Good Huswifes Handmaide for the Kitchin (1594)

To make a blanch manger on the fish day. Take the whites of eggs and cream, and boil them on a chafing dish on coals, till they curd; then will their whey go from them. Then put away the whey, then put to the curd a little rosewater, then strain it and season it with sugar.

The Second Part of the Good Huswifes Jewell (1597)

Cider syllabub

'A posset or selibub made of verjuice is good to cool a choleric stomach', writes Thomas Cogan in *The Haven of Health*; 'cider syllabubs' are among the good things enjoyed at Maid Marion's sheep-shearing feast in Ben Jonson's *The Sad Shepherd*. Cider and verjuice were typical ingredients, but wines such as 'sherris sack' (sherry) could replace them. Syllabub emerges from almost nowhere into sixteenth-century English literature. The word occurs in no other language and its origin is obscure.

As Cogan implies, posset and syllabub are much alike in their ingredients. The difference is that in posset the cream is warmed, while syllabub is made without heat.

Shakespeare never mentions cider, though the setting of Falstaff's comfortable meal with Shallow, in an apple orchard in Gloucestershire, is a strong hint at the existence of this beverage. Cider, writes Charles Estienne in Paris in 1550, is 'rather good for the digestion if made from fully ripe apples that are carefully washed, if they are gathered in season and stored as long as necessary. Some excellent apple varieties, particularly suitable for cider-making, have more juice after maturing and storage'. Estienne thinks of Normandy and Maine as cider-producing regions, while his near-contemporary Thomas Cogan, writing in London, looks to the English West Country: 'Cider is not in so common use anywhere in this land as in Worcestershire and Gloucestershire', he comments, adding that it is 'good for them that have hot stomachs or hot livers. Yet if it be used for a common drink . . . it maketh even in youth the colour of the face pale and the skin rivelled.' There was even a story, current in Shakespeare's lifetime, that in the year 1216 King John's fatal illness had been exacerbated by 'evil surfeiting and naughty diet, by eating peaches and drinking of new cider'.

[Cyder.] You shall take every apple by itself, and looking upon them, pick them clean from all manner of filthiness, as bruisings, rottenness, worm-eating, and such like. Which done you shall put them into some very clean trough, and, with beetles made for the purpose, bruise or crush the apples: then take a bag of hair-cloth, and filling it full of the crushed fruit, put it in a press of wood, and press out all the juice, and so bagful after bagful cease not until you have pressed all. As soone as your liquor is pressed forth and hath stood to settle about twelve hours you shall then tun it up into sweet hogsheads, as those which have had in

Red ſtreak

Frontispiece to *Vinetum Britannicum: or A treatise of cider, and other wines and drinks extracted from fruits growing in this kingdom*, by John Worlidge (fl. 1669–98), published in 1678. Folger Shakespeare Library.

them last either white wine or claret, as for the sack vessel it is tolerable but not excellent, and this being done you shall clay up the bung-hole with clay and salt mixed together, so close as is possible.

Gervase Markham, The English Husbandman (1613), abridged

To make an excellent sillibubbe. Fill your syllabub pot with cider, and good store of sugar, and a little nutmeg, stir it well together, and when the sugar is melted, put in as much cream, by 2 or 3 spoonfuls at a time. Then stir it softly once about, let it stand 2 hours at least before it be eaten: the standing makes it curdle.

Mrs. Sarah Longe her Receipt Booke (c. 1610)

Cider

Making cider at home is a good idea if you have more apples than you can eat. The processes are these: wash and chop the apples (no need to peel or core them); shred, pulp or grind them to release the juice; press them; leave the juice to ferment, for about one to three weeks depending on the temperature, not sealing the vessel but covering it; when the fermentation dies down, rack the new cider off the lees into a clean vessel which must be full and must be closed with an airlock to exclude air. When the slow fermentation stops the cider can be bottled. If you make cider this way it will be dry and will probably contain 5–8 per cent alcohol.

Any and all apples can be used but some will give much better flavour and keeping qualities than others. Unless you have a particularly good variety the best results will come from a blend of apples including acid as well as sweet. Use ripe apples, because the more sugar, the more alcohol, and the stronger your cider, the better it keeps. If you are not satisfied with the flavour, you can try killing the natural yeast (with Campden tablets) and replacing it with a wine yeast. Before bottling it is best to test with a cidrometer, because, if there is residual sugar, bottle fermentation will start in the spring. A little of this gives sparkle; a lot of it leads to explosions. It can be prevented if you sterilize with Campden tablets before bottling (in which case you can add 'contains sulfites' to your label: you are not alone!).

Cider syllabub

If you are buying cider for this syllabub recipe, try the effect of medium and sweet ciders. If you make your own, and it is dry, you may want to add more sugar.

110 ml/3³/₄ fl oz/¹/₂ cup medium cider
3 teaspoons soft brown sugar
220 ml/8 fl oz/1 cup double cream
Nutmeg to taste

Leave the sugar to dissolve in the cider for about 10 minutes. Pour in the cream and whisk with an electric mixer until it thickens and stands in soft peaks. Serve in individual glasses, dusted with the nutmeg.

Sliced oranges

Lady Gula in this text is not a secret friend of Thomas Cogan. *Gula* is the Latin for 'throat', and 'Lady Gula' is just another way of saying 'fashionable gastronomy'. Cogan is telling us that the Elizabethans already had the idea of garnishing roast meat with slices of orange, and also of serving slices of orange, sprinkled with sugar, as a sticky finger food.

[A banqueting dish.] The substance of the orange is used to be eaten raw with roasted flesh, as a sauce . . . Lady Gula hath not only commended them to be eaten with meats, but also devised a banquetting dish to be made with sliced oranges and sugar cast upon them.

Thomas Cogan, *The Haven of Health* (1636)

Shakespeare's rivals

When Shakespeare began to write for the London stage he was moving into a crowded field. Omitting Christopher Marlowe and other major contemporaries, we mention here only the playwrights who happen to be quoted in this book for their references to food and festivity.

Robert Greene, Master of Arts of both universities as he proudly claimed, had some reason to resent the intrusion of a grammar-school boy. Greene wrote comedies with historical settings, including the very popular *Friar Bacon and Friar Bungay*, printed in 1594, and others that were successful but soon forgotten. Greene wrote assiduously in many genres. His fable (it can hardly be called a novel) *Pandosto* gave Shakespeare the theme and setting for *The Winter's Tale*. His success (unlike Shakespeare's) was not the kind that brings wealth, and he apparently died penniless in 1592.

Ben Jonson, like Greene and with more justification though he never went to university, regarded himself as a scholar. Eight years younger than Shakespeare, he found a first niche as a writer for the public stage, and a second more comfortable one as an author of masques for King James I's court. Like Shakespeare he also acted on occasion. Jonson achieved great popularity with comedies such as *Bartholomew Fair* and *Every Man in his Humour*, both of them rewarding reads for the food historian; his toga plays such as *Sejanus's Fall* were less admired and he was sometimes in trouble with the censors. He was nasty in private about Shakespeare's work; his older rival 'wanted art and sometimes sense', Jonson is reported to have said, giving the plot of *The Winter's Tale* as an example. He it was who alleged that Shakespeare had 'small Latin and less Greek', which, compared with Jonson himself, is certainly true. But this last quotation is taken from Jonson's memorial poem to Shakespeare, printed in the First Folio, and that poem is a generous and perceptive tribute to a rival whom Jonson knew to have been far more successful than himself. *The Sad Shepherd*, which we quote alongside *The Winter's Tale* because they both feature a sheep-shearing feast, was Jonson's last play, left unfinished at his death in 1637.

Thomas Middleton, an Oxford student who never graduated, was sixteen years younger than Shakespeare and began to write for the theatre in 1603. He was successful with history plays, tragedies and comedies; he had a long quarrel with Jonson; he may have worked with Shakespeare on *Timon of Athens*. We quote from the banquet scene in *The Witch*: Middleton wrote this play for the King's Servants in order to build on a fashion for witchcraft – a fashion that Shakespeare had started. Witches' songs from *The Witch* were eventually included in the standard First Folio version of *Macbeth*. Jonson used the same theme again, with vast learning and endless footnotes, in his *The Masque of Queens*, performed at court in 1609 with a cast of princesses and duchesses. Readers searching for recipes for witches' brews will find them here.

John Fletcher, best known for his collaborations with Francis Beaumont, was a close contemporary of Middleton. While Middleton remained a 'freelance', Fletcher took over Shakespeare's position as regular writer for the King's Men. It seems that the two worked together for a while: Fletcher's style is identified in some parts of *King Henry VIII*, the play that provides a theme for chapter 7 of this book. We have cited Beaumont and Fletcher's tragedy *Cupid's Revenge*, written some time before 1612, in discussing the recipe for baked warden pear. The line we quote, from act 2 scene 3, is usually attributed to Fletcher.

Food books of Shakespeare's time

Printing spread across Europe in the late fifteenth century. It reached Rome in 1467, Venice in 1469, Paris in 1470, Lyon in 1473, London (or rather Westminster, with William Caxton) in 1476. In all these places it was not long before books about food began to be printed. The first landmark is Bartolomeo Platina's unexpectedly readable little handbook of food and nutrition, *De honesta voluptate et valetudine* ('On proper pleasure and good health'), written in Rome where Platina was Papal librarian, published in Venice in 1475.

Our focus in this book is England, but we quote from a few relevant foreign publications of Shakespeare's time. The oldest text that we quote is the recipe book *Epulario* ('The banqueter' or 'The banquet book'), which appeared in Venice in 1517: too early and too distant to be within our scope, but it was reissued in Venice in 1596 and soon afterwards appeared in an English translation, published in London in 1598. We used the 1596 edition.

In 1604 (the same year in which *Othello* was performed) appeared a cookery book compiled by Lancelot de Casteau, master cook in the service of three successive prince-bishops of the once autonomous city of Liège, now in Belgium. For comparison's sake we quote from a couple of Casteau's recipes, one for a veal hodgepot – with capers – and one for a *potage*. We also quote from Charles Estienne's Latin handbook of food and nutrition, *De nutrimentis*, published by his family press in Paris in 1550. Estienne's books were popular among Latinists, especially students, and they certainly circulated in England.

The earliest English food book that we use here is Sir Thomas Elyot's *The Castel of Helth*, first published in 1533. We quote from the 1541 edition, which was reprinted later in the century. Elyot is best known as a diplomat involved in the difficult international negotiations over Henry VIII's divorce from Catherine of Aragon, and as an educationalist, author of *The Book called the Governor*. His *Castel of Helth* is a short text based on Greek and Latin diet handbooks (as is Charles Estienne's work) but it also shows evidence of independence. Andrew Boorde, who published *A Compendyous Regyment* in 1542, nearly became a bishop, turned to medicine (which he studied at Montpellier), was also briefly a political emissary, and is said to have been imprisoned in London in 1549 for keeping a brothel. The other authors of sixteenth-century English food books had less exciting lives. William Bullein, author of *The Government of Health* (1558, reissued

in 1595), wrote about religion as well as diet; Thomas Cogan, a native of Somerset, became a fellow of Oriel College, Oxford, and for some years Master of Manchester Grammar School. Evidently Cogan was well qualified, at least by experience, to compile a health handbook *'chiefly gathered for the comfort of students'*: that is the focus of *The Haven of Health*, which appeared in 1584. We quote it from the fourth edition of 1636. We have also used Tobias Venner's *Via recta ad vitam longam* (1620): Venner, too, was a Somerset man, author of the first book ever published on the health benefits of *The Baths of Bath*.

As with diet and nutrition, writing about botanical and agricultural sciences had flourished on the continent before it spread in the later sixteenth century to England. We have quoted occasionally from the *New Herbal*, a 1578 English translation of the 1564 Dutch *Cruydeboeck*, an illustrated manual of plants and their uses. This was the great work of Rembert Dodoens, who ended his career as professor of medicine at Leiden. The English translator, Henry Lyte, is our third Somerset author. We have also quoted from a household and farming book, *Maison rustique, or, The Countrie Farme*. This was first published in Latin in 1554 by Charles Estienne; expanded in French translation in 1564 by Jean Liébault; revised and translated into English by Richard Surflet in 1600; then expanded again in a second English edition, by the industrious hack writer Gervase Markham, in 1616. We have used two other books by Markham, *The English Husbandman* and *The English Housewife*, both published shortly before Shakespeare's death.

For the recipes in this book we draw on several cookbooks printed between 1573 and 1596. This was the first great flourish of recipe books in English publishing: indeed there had hardly been such concentrated publishing activity in this subject area anywhere in Europe. We use *A Proper Newe Booke of Cokerye*, first published 1545, reissued 1575; *A Book of Cookrye very necessary for all such as delight therin*, first published 1584, reissued 1591; *The Good Huswifes Handmaide for the Kitchin*, first published 1594, reissued 1597. All these are general cookbooks by unknown authors, though the *Book of Cookrye* is credited to a certain 'A.W.'. It was into this same small pond that the English translation of the Italian *Epulario* was launched in 1598.

In addition to these general cookbooks we use some more specialized recipe books focusing on sweets and preserves. As if to demonstrate that this topic is of especial value to the reader and needs to be learned from an expert, these books all have cleverly devised titles and all but one are credited to named authors: John Partridge's *The Treasurie of Commodious Conceits* (1573), Thomas Dawson's *The Good Huswifes Jewell* (1585) and Sir Hugh Plat's *Delightes for Ladies* (1602). Whether Thomas Dawson also wrote *The Second Part of the Good Hus-wives Jewell* (1597), or whether his publisher reused his title, we are not certain.

The cookbooks

A Proper Newe Booke of Cokerye. First published 1545. Online transcription by Daniel Myers of the 1575 edition at www.medievalcookery.com/notes/ pnboc1575.txt

The Commonplace Book of Countess Katherine Seymour Hertford [Lady Catherine Grey], died 1568. Manuscript in the University of Pennsylvania Library. Online transcription by Daniel Myers at www.medievalcookery. com/notes/mscodex823.txt

John Partridge, *The Treasurie of Commodious Conceits*. First published 1573; several later editions. Online edition by Johnna Holloway at www.medievalcookery.com/notes/ treasurie.pdf

A.W., *A Book of Cookrye very necessary for all such as delight therin*. First published 1584; new edition 1591. Online transcription by Mark and Jane Waks of the 1591 edition at jducoeur.org/Cookbook/Cookrye.html

Thomas Dawson, *The Good Huswifes Jewell*. First published 1585; new edition 1596. Online transcription by Daniel Myers of the 1596 edition at www.medievalcookery. com/notes/ghj1596.txt. See also the edition by Maggie Black (2002), cited in the Further reading, page 141.

The Good Huswifes Handmaide for the Kitchin. First published 1594; new edition 1597. Online transcription by Sam Wallace, hosted by Thomas Gloning, based on the 1594 edition at www.uni-giessen.de/gloning/ghhk/

The Second Part of the Good Hus-wives Jewell. 1597. Online transcription hosted by Abigail Weiner at home.comcast. net/~morwenna/Cooks/dawson2.html

Epulario, or The Italian Banquet. 1598. A translation of the Italian *Epulario*, by Giovanni de Rosselli (first published 1517, republished 1596)

Hugh Plat, *Delightes for Ladies*. 1602. Online transcription of the 1609 printing at www.havaris.ca/1/ delightsforladies/

Mrs. Sarah Longe her Receipt Booke (*c*. 1610). Manuscript in the Folger Shakespeare Library. Edition by Rachel Doggett and E. Dever Powell, with introduction by Heidi Brayman Hackel, in *Fooles and Fricassees* (see Further reading, page 141).

John Murrell, *A New Booke of Cookerie*. First published 1615; facsimile, 1972. Online transcription by Thomas Gloning at www.uni-giessen.de/gloning/tx/1615murr. htm.

The dietary texts

Andrew Boorde, *A Compendyous Regyment or a Dyetary of Helth*. First published 1542. Edited by F.J. Furnivall in 1870 under the title *The fyrst boke of the introduction of knowledge*. Reading copy of the 1870 edition at www. archive.org/details/fyrstbokeofintro00boorrich

William Bullein, *The Government of Health*. First published 1558; new edition 1595.

Thomas Cogan, *The Haven of Health: chiefly gathered for the comfort of students*. First published 1584; 4th edition 1636. Reading copy of the 1636 edition at http://www. archive.org/details/havenofhealthchi00coga

Thomas Elyot, *The Castel of Helth*. First published 1533; new edition 1541; often reprinted. Reading copy of the 1541 edition at www.archive.org/details/ castelofhelthcor00elyoiala

William Langham, *The Garden of Health*. First published 1579; new edition 1633.

Tobias Venner, *Via recta ad vitam longam*. First published 1620.

Further reading

To find all of Shakespeare's references to food, or to any particular foodstuff, the starting point is Joan Fitzpatrick's *Shakespeare and the Language of Food: a Dictionary* (London 2011). This also contains many quotations from contemporary and slightly later books on food, diet and health.

The relation between Renaissance food writing and Renaissance beliefs about health is now a well-studied field. It is the focus of another recent book by Joan Fitzpatrick, *Food in Shakespeare: early modern dietaries and the plays* (London 2007); also of Ken Albala's *Eating right in the Renaissance* (Berkeley 2002); and, in part, of Robert Appelbaum's engaging study, *Aguecheek's beef, Belch's hiccup and other gastronomic interjections* (Chicago 2006). It may be unfair to characterize these wide-ranging books in such a simple way, but Fitzpatrick begins from Shakespearean talk, Albala from dietary thought both European and English. Appelbaum starts, as you would expect from the title, with *Twelfth Night* and Sir Andrew Aguecheek's fears about the deleterious effect of beef on his wit (see page 64).

There are several more wide-ranging books on food and dining in Shakespeare's time. Closest to the subject is Alison Sim's *Food and feast in Tudor England* (Stroud 1997). A general approach, taking in Europe as well as England, is offered in Ken Albala's *Food in early modern Europe* (Westport 2003). Ken Albala, again, is the author of *The banquet: dining in the great courts of late Renaissance Europe* (Urbana IL 2007). His subject-matter here ranges wider than banquets and great courts. Joan Fitzpatrick, again, edited the collection of essays *Renaissance food from Rabelais to Shakespeare: culinary readings and culinary histories* (London 2010). Shakespeare bulks much larger in this collection than Rabelais. Tracy Thong's essay surveys banquet scenes in Shakespeare (omitting *King Henry VIII*) and other Renaissance dramatists; but there's more, a whole book on banquets in Tudor and Stuart plays, Chris Meads's *Banquets set forth* (Manchester 2001).

Banquets, whether dessert course or independent meal, are the whole subject of a collection edited by C. Anne Wilson, *Banqueting stuffe: the fare and social background of the Tudor and Stuart banquet* (Edinburgh 1991). Anyone wanting to recreate a Tudor banquet needs this book. Anyone working on Tudor food and dining needs *Fooles and fricassees: food in Shakespeare's England* (Seattle 2000). Edited by Mary Anne Caton, this is an exhibition catalogue based on the collections of the Folger Shakespeare Library. The book's only fault, considering its subtitle, is that many of the exhibits described and illustrated date from well after Shakespeare's death, but the introductory essay by Joan Thirsk, also entitled 'Food in Shakespeare's England', is indispensable.

Turning to cookbooks, three that were written in England in Shakespeare's time but remained in manuscript have been made available quite recently. The first of these was published as *Elinor Fettiplace's receipt book: Elizabethan country house cooking*, edited by Hilary Spurling (London 1986). The second, a manuscript in the Folger Shakespeare Library, is edited as an appendix to *Fooles and fricassees* (see above): it is *Mrs. Sarah Longe her Receipt Booke*, dated to about 1610; we have quoted several recipes from it, including Mrs Longe's gooseberry fool. The third has recently appeared online in Daniel Myers's transcription (see 'The cookbooks' above): it forms part of the *Commonplace Book* of Lady Catherine Grey, a manuscript in the University of Pennsylvania Library. The owner of this book, a tragic figure, was the sister of Jane Grey (who was placed on the English throne in 1553, was immediately supplanted by Elizabeth I, and was executed in 1554. Catherine secretly married Edward Seymour, Earl of Hertford, in 1560. Elizabeth regarded her as the possible founder of a rival dynasty and ordered her imprisonment when the fact of the marriage became known. The marriage was eventually annulled and the children rendered illegitimate. Catherine Grey died in 1568, still a prisoner, at the age of twenty-seven. The manuscript contains a deathbed statement by her, as well as recipes for foods, conserves and medicines.

One of the cookery books published during Shakespeare's lifetime, Thomas Dawson's *The Good Housewife's Jewel*, has appeared recently in a new edition, edited and with an introduction by Maggie Black (Lewes 2002).

We know of five other historical cookbooks that link the name of Shakespeare with their recipes, each taking a slightly different approach. They are: Domenica De Rosa, *The little book of Shakespeare and food* (New York 2001); Madge Lorwin, *Dining with William Shakespeare: thirteen complete Shakespearean feast menus* (New York 1976); Mark Morton, *Cooking with Shakespeare* (New York 2008); Francine Segan, *Shakespeare's kitchen: Renaissance recipes for the contemporary cook* (New York 2003); and Betty Zyvatkaukas, *Eating Shakespeare* (New York 2002).

Quotations and references

Shakespeare's plays are quoted throughout by title alone, without act, scene and line numbers. To find the full context of any quotation, the most useful website is gutenberg.org, which gives in modern spelling the whole text of each play on a single page.

For the recipe books and dietary and herbal texts quoted throughout, see the lists on page 140.

Introduction R. Greene, *Greene's groat's worth of wit* (1592); F. Meres, *Palladis tamia* (1598); R. Greene, *Friar Bacon and Friar Bungay* (*c.* 1588–92); W. Bullein, *The Government of Health* (1595), quoted in J. Fitzpatrick, *Shakespeare and the language of food* (2011), 393; W. Langham, *The Garden of Health* (1633), 125; *Epulario* (1596), 31–2; C. Estienne, *De nutrimentis* (1550), 72–3; *The Commonplace Book of Countess Katherine Seymour Hertford* at www.medievalcookery.com; T. Middleton, *Women beware women* (1626), act 3 scene 3; W. Bullein, *Bullein's bulwark of defence* (1579), quoted in F.J. Furnivall, *Early English meals and manners* (1868), 91; G. Markham, *The English husbandman* (1613), part 2, ch. 9, quoted at www.gutenberg.org/ebooks/22973; British Library, MS Harleian 642 (1625), in *A collection of ordinances and regulations for the government of the Royal Household* (1790), 300; C. Estienne, J. Liébault (tr. Richard Surflet), *Maison rustique, or, The Countrie Farme* (1600); Virgil, *Aeneid*, book 7, line 116; W. Caxton (tr.), *Eneydos* (1490); J. Smith, *The generall historie of Virginia, New-England, and the Summer Isles* (1624).

1 'Save me a piece of marchpane!' *Historia novellamente ritrovata di due nobili amanti* (1530); G. Markham, *The English huswife* (1615), quoted in J. Fitzpatrick, *Shakespeare and the language of food* (2011), 55; *Establishment of Prince Henry* (1610), in *A collection of ordinances and regulations for the government of the Royal Household* (1790), 317; W. Bullein, *The Government of Health* (1595), quoted in J. Fitzpatrick, *Shakespeare and the language of food* (2011), 55; R. Surflet, G. Markham, *Maison rustique or The countrie farme* (1616), 585; H. Plat, *Delights for Ladies* (1609), no. 18, 'To make a marchpane'; R. Fabyan, *The concordance of histories* (1515; 1811 edn), 586; J. Nichols, *The Progresses and Public Processions of Queen Elizabeth I*, I (1823), xxxvi–ii.

2 'The dinner attends you' Erasmus, *Colloquies*; quoted in T. Cogan, *The Haven of Health*.

3 'I am a great eater of beef' J. Manningham, Diary, 2 February 1602, quoted in B.R. Smith, *William Shakespeare: Twelfth night or What you will: texts and contexts* (2001), 2; K. Digby, *The Closet of Sir Kenelm Digby Opened* (1669), quoted in Stephenson and Davidson edn (1997); L. de Casteau, *Ouverture de cuisine* (1604); J. Palsgrave, *L'éclaircissement de la langue française* (1530), 202; Bible (King James Version, 1611), Exodus 12:39; N. Breton, *Pasquil's fool's-cap* (1600); *Sir Giles Goosecap* (1606).

4 'The funeral baked meats' A. Dumas and P. Meurice (tr.), *Hamlet, prince de Danemark* (1849); K. Digby, *The Closet of Sir Kenelm Digby Opened* (1669), quoted in Stephenson and Davidson edn (1997); Bible (King James Version, 1611), Genesis 40:16–17; *The image of hypocrisy*, lines 1173–8, quoted in F.J. Furnivall, ed., *Ballads from Manuscripts*, I (1868), 218; F. Beaumont and J. Fletcher, *Cupid's revenge* (1612), act 2; *Potages dyvers* (*c.* 1430), in T. Austin, ed., *Two fifteenth-century cookery-books* (1888), 51; T. Venner, *Via recta ad vitam longam* (1620), 41.

5 'Fail not our feast' R. Holinshed, *Chronicles of England, Scotland and Ireland*, II (1577), 243; T. Middleton, *The Witch* (1616); W. Turner, *Herbal*, III (1568), 71.

6 'Our sheep-shearing feast' R. Greene, *Greene's groat's worth of wit* (1592); R. Greene, *Pandosto* (1588); A.M. Stirling, 'Holkham: a famous sheep-shearing feast' (1908), repr. in A.L.J. Gosset, ed., *Shepherds of Britain* (1911), 214–16; B. Jonson, *The sad shepherd* (before 1637); T. Elyot, *The boke named the Governour* (1531), quoted in the *Oxford English Dictionary*; T. Elyot, *The Castel of Helth* (1541), book 2, ch. 14, 'Of grapes and raisins'.

7 'An idle banquet' R. Holinshed, *Chronicles of England, Scotland and Ireland*, VI (2nd edn, 1587), 893; H. Wotton, letter of 2 July 1613, in L. Pearsall Smith, ed., *The life and letters of Sir Henry Wotton*, II (1907), 32–3; J. Foxe, *The acts and monuments of the Christian Church* (1563, 1576), ch. 48; H. Lyte, 'A description of the swans of Carie', in *Notes and queries*, 6th ser. VIII (1883), 109–10; C. Estienne, *De nutrimentis* (1550), 22–3.

Index

Picture credits

All British Museum images are © The Trustees of the British Museum, courtesy of the Museum's Department of Photography and Imaging. The numbers listed below refer to the page numbers of illustrations from other collections.

14 The State Hermitage Museum, St Petersburg / The Bridgeman Art Library
19 Museo del Prado, Madrid / Giraudon / The Bridgeman Art Library
79 By permission of the Folger Shakespeare Library
95 Musée des Beaux-Arts, Reims / Giraudon / The Bridgeman Art Library
135 By permission of the Folger Shakespeare Library